The Ministry of Music

Other Books by Kenneth W. Osbeck

Amazing Grace: *366 Hymn Stories for Daily Devotions*
Devotional Warm-ups for the Church Choir
52 Hymn Stories *Dramatized*
Junior's Praise
My Music Workbook
Pocket Guide for the Church Choir Member
101 Hymn Stories
101 More Hymn Stories
The Endless Song: *Music and Worship in the Church*

The Ministry of Music

by
KENNETH W. OSBECK

Foreword by
JOHN L. MILES

Grand Rapids, MI 49501

Library of Congress Catalog Card No. 61-14865

ISBN 0-8254-3410-6 (paperback)

10 11 12 Printing / Year 99 98 97 96 95

Printed in the United States of America

CONTENTS

Maintenance; Rehearsal Techniques; Matters of Performance; Group Musicianship; Lack of Sight Reading Ability; Lack of Confident Singing; Poor Intonation; Poor Blend; Poor Diction; Lack of Proper Balance; Ineffective Interpretation; Materials; Criteria for Choosing New Music; Program Building; Gospel Song and Hymn Arrangement Collections; Anthem Collections; 25 Selected Anthems; Several of the Standard Cantatas and Longer Works for Passion and Advent Seasons

FOREWORD

The attention of the church is being focused more and more on the music department and its ministry. Great changes are taking place in the field of Christian music and these changes are affecting the work of the church. It is time for all Christians to examine every phase of sacred music to determine if present trends and changes are harmful or beneficial and to see if we are truly glorifying the Lord in our use of music.

Any investigation, to be of value, must cover all phases: History, spiritual concepts and convictions upon which one can build, an analysis of trends, practical suggestions for working with various age groups, suggested materials, etc. Mr. Osbeck has covered all of these areas in this study. The author's educational background, his years of teaching at the Grand Rapids School of the Bible and Music, and his capable leadership with all types of church music groups make him well qualified to examine and draw conclusions about the ministry of music.

I am certain this book is a timely and much needed contribution to the present literature available on the subject of improving the music program in evangelical churches.

John L. Miles, *Former President,*
Grand Rapids School of the Bible and Music

PREFACE

"Praise ye the Lord: for it is good to sing praises unto our God; for it is pleasant; and praise is comely [proper]."
Psalm 147:1

This book has been prepared for the purpose of aiding those in Christian service and those preparing for Christian leadership to have a better understanding of the possibilities and benefits of a vital music program in the local evangelical church.

Once again, after revising and updating this material for publication of another edition, I am grateful to God for His hand of past blessing upon this work. The book has been widely used for more than two decades in schools both in this country and abroad in training men and women for the music ministry. It has also proven to be a helpful resource book for many individual church music leaders.

It is my sincere prayer and desire that God will continue to use this new edition to quicken in each Christian music leader a total dedication of talent and life as well as a deeper perception of the spiritual purposes of sacred music. Together may our musical ministries count mightily for God to reach needy souls with the glorious truths of the Gospel.

KENNETH W. OSBECK

Grand Rapids, Michigan

ACKNOWLEDGMENTS

The author wishes to acknowledge the contributions and inspiration of those who have made this work possible. This includes many authors of books and articles, my students and fellow teachers, as well as those of all ages who have shared in the music ministry in the various churches in which I have been privileged to minister.

INTRODUCTION

From the time of Old Testament Hebrew worship and through-out church history, music has been one of the important influences in the work of God. When one considers the role of the New Testament church in providing opportunities for worship, evangelism, edification and fellowship in today's society, one can readily realize that music is still one of the vital means available for the local assembly to achieve these God-given objectives. Regardless of one's particular field of endeavor in Christian service, music has a major role. It is important, therefore, that any pastor, music director, music committee member, or any lay person involved with the leadership of any public service or special group learn all that he/she can about this phase of church life.

This basic understanding of the music ministry for any church leader should include instruction in such areas as a knowledge of the historical growth of sacred music, an awareness of the necessary qualification of music leaders, the development of basic skills for leading congregational singing and services of worship, as well as the ability to administer and direct special groups such as children's choirs, youth-teens, adults and instrumental groups, and possibly assist in a radio ministry.

The term "evangelical church" in this book means a church that believes and teaches the Bible as God's infallible and inspired Word. It is a church that adheres to the basic tenets of the historic Christian faith. It is a church with a zealous evangelistic and missionary emphasis, challenging individuals with the necessity of the new birth — a personal response of faith in the redemptive work of Jesus Christ. It is a church that desires to lead its believers into a life of yieldedness to the Holy Spirit and in turn a life of service in the work of the Lord.

There is a greater need in our evangelical churches today for musical leadership, both on the professional and lay levels, than has ever before existed. Opportunities are unlimited — choirs and ensembles for every age group and instrumental, handbell, drama activities — all of which will add immeasurably to the spiritual

dynamic of any church. Praying and praising are still true ther-
mometers of the spiritual health of individual believers as well as
of local assemblies.

> God sent His singers upon the earth
> With songs of sadness and of mirth,
> That they might touch the hearts of men
> And bring them back to heaven again.
>
> "The Singers" by Henry Wadsworth Longfellow

The Ministry of Music

1 | THE HISTORICAL DEVELOPMENT OF SACRED MUSIC

I. BEFORE THE TIME OF CHRIST

Man is basically a religious though unregenerate being. In all human life there is a consciousness of a supreme power. Even the most primitive savage is a religious being as he attempts to fulfill his duties to the invisible powers he senses about him. Since the beginning of recorded time, music has always had a unique association with man's worship experiences.

There has been much evidence uncovered that the Egyptian culture, one of the earliest known, made extensive use of music in religious rites. The Egyptians possessed many musical instruments, from the little tinkling sistrums to the ornamented harps of twelve or thirteen strings. Undoubtedly Greece, the next important culture in early human history, gained musical knowledge and practice from the Egyptians.

The Greeks made extensive use of music in their religious rituals and also ascribed to it an influence over the moral and emotional nature of man and credited its origin to their gods. In his writings concerning music, Plutarch says: "The right moulding of ingenuous manners and civil conduct lies in a well-grounded musical education."

Although the Hebrews used music in their worship of Jehovah, it was never developed to the extent that it was under Grecian influence, where notation and the entire organization of a musical system first took form. The Hebrews, unlike the Greeks, did not associate music with morality or with magical properties. For the Hebrew, the arts obtained significance only as they could be used to adorn the courts of Jehovah or could be employed in the ascription of praise to Him.

Most of what is known about the use of music in Hebrew worship is learned from the Old Testament. Here numerous references are found to prove the importance of both vocal and instrumental music in Hebrew worship. The first mention of music

17

in the Bible is found in Genesis 4:21, where Jubal is spoken of as "the father of all such as handle the harp and pipe." In the Scriptures there are about thirteen different instruments mentioned, which can be classified as stringed instruments, wind instruments or instruments of percussion. There are a number of singers and songs mentioned in the Old Testament. For example:

Miriam's Song, Exodus 15:20-21.
Moses' Song, Exodus 15:2.
The Song of Deborah and Barak, Judges 5:3.
Hannah's Song of Thankfulness, I Samuel 2:1-10.
David's Song of Thanksgiving and Deliverance from Saul, II Samuel 22.

Altogether, the words "music," "musicians," "musical instruments," "song," "singers" and "singing" appear 575 times in the complete Bible. References to music are found in 44 of the 66 books in the Bible. One entire book, the Psalms, containing 150 chapters, is believed to have been in its original form a book of songs.

With the capture of Jerusalem under David and the permanent establishment of the Tabernacle at that city, the worship service increased greatly in splendor and musical display. Part of an entire priestly tribe, the Levites, were commissioned with the task of providing musical instruction and leadership for these services. Under King David's leadership the first large choir and orchestra were organized for use in the Tabernacle worship.

When Solomon, David's son, became king and built the first temple, the splendor and musical display of the worship services increased even more. The third chapter of the eighth book of Josephus, the Jewish historian, states that in this first temple there were 200,000 trumpets and 200,000 robed singers trained for taking part in these services. The fifth chapter of II Chronicles gives an interesting account of a large group of singers and instrumentalists, arrayed in white linen gowns, taking part in the service. The climax of the service came when both united in one glorious expression of praise:

"It came to pass, as the trumpeters and singers were as one, to make one sound to be heard in praising and thanking the Lord; and when they lifted up their voice with the trumpets and cymbals and instruments of musick, and praised the Lord, saying, For He is good; for His mercy endureth for ever: that then the house was filled with a cloud, even the house of the Lord; So that the priests could not stand to minister by the reason of the cloud; for the glory of the Lord had filled the house of God" (II Chronicles 5:13, 14).

Following the return from Babylonian captivity, temple worship was once again restored to the Hebrews with the building of the second temple. Although this temple was not as elaborate as the first, there is evidence that musical grandeur and display had an important role in these services as well. The Jewish Talmud describes the traditions of the psalm singing of this second temple. It states that when a sign was given on the cymbals, twelve Levites stood upon the broad step of a stairway leading from the place of the congregation to the outer court of the priests and played upon nine lyres, two harps and one cymbal. While they did so, the priests poured out the wine offering. Younger Levites played other instruments but did not sing. Still other Levitical boys added their voices to the treble part but did not play instruments. The pauses of the psalm, or its divisions or selahs, were indicated by blasts of trumpets at the right and left of the cymbalists.

II. The Birth of Jesus Christ

With the advent of a new era at the birth of Jesus Christ, a new spirit and a new motive, unknown to the earlier Egyptian, Greek, Roman or Hebrew cultures, pervaded religious consciousness. It was a spirit of joy, a joy of having a personal and intimate relationship with God through the person and redemptive work of His Son, Jesus Christ. No longer was worship confined to the temple or synagogue, but rather each believer himself became a temple of the living God. This was not a joy of hilarity and rhythmic demonstrations as in the primitive religions. It was a joy tempered with a deep sense of personal unworthiness, awe and intense devotion to the Person of Christ.

Although much of the church worship had to be done in secret because of Roman oppressors, nevertheless music was a natural expression for this newly found Christian joy. Church history records many incidents of early Christians marching triumphantly to their martyrdom singing hymns of praise about their Saviour. The fact that music was used extensively in the early Apostolic and Post-Apostolic churches can be learned from such New Testament references as Ephesians 5:19, Colossians 3:16, Acts 16:25, and James 5:13. Other testimony regarding the use of music by early Christians is contained in the celebrated letter of the younger Pliny from Bithynia to the Emperor Trajan, in the year 112 A.D., in which the Christians are described as coming together before daylight and singing hymns to Christ.

As had been true in the worship services of ancient Judaism, the chief source of early Christian music was the Psalms. In addition to this, however, there was the use of texts such as Mary's song, the Magnificat — "My Soul Doth Magnify the Lord . . . ," Luke 1:46-55; the song of Zacharias, the Benedictus — "Blessed Be the Lord God of Israel . . . ," Luke 1:68-79; The Angels' Song, Gloria in Excelsis — "Glory to God in the Highest . . . ," Luke 2:14; Simeon's Song, Nunc Dimittis — "Lord Now Lettest Thou Thy Servant Depart in Peace . . . ," Luke 2:29; the singing of Jesus — "And When They Had Sung an Hymn . . . ,"Matthew 26:30. Other songs mentioned in the New Testament include the singing of Paul and Silas, Acts 16:25, and the future songs of the redeemed, Revelation 14:3 and 15:3. The music of the early Christian churches was entirely vocal, with little regard for instruments of any kind. In fact, the early church fathers, such as Clement of Alexandria, St. Chrysostom, St. Ambrose, St. Augustine, strongly denounced the use of instruments with sacred singing.

With the legalizing of Christianity in 313 A.D. under Constantine the Great, the simple organization of the apostolic churches gradually developed into a complex system of liturgy and ritual. The clergy were no longer the servants or representatives of the people, but held a mediatorial position as the channels through which divine grace was transmitted to the faithful. During these early years of the Christian church, St. Ambrose of Milan, born at Treves, France about 340 A.D., did much to encourage congregational singing. Gradually, however, the individual worshiper assumed more and more the role of a passive onlooker rather than that of an active participant, as the clergy assumed charge of nearly all of the details in this liturgical service, including the musical portion of the service.

III. THE MIDDLE AGES OR MEDIEVAL PERIOD

The next one thousand year period, covering a span of time roughly from the fourth century to the Renaissance-Reformation period, is generally spoken of by historians as the "Middle-Ages," "Medieval Period," or the "Dark Ages." The chants or plain songs performed by the priests are the most important musical development of the church from the fourth through the sixth centuries. The exact origin of these chants is unknown. The church's next important musical leader was St. Gregory the Great toward the close of the sixth century. The chants or plain songs of this time are often referred to as "Gregorian Chants."

The ensuing years, from the seventh century to the time of

the Renaissance-Reformation, witnessed many important musical activities and developments. The liturgy of the Mass was definitely established. This consisted of two main parts: the Mass Ordinary or the unchanging portions of the Mass and the Mass Proper or the variable portions of each Mass. The Mass Ordinary consisted of five main divisions: the Kyrie, Credo, Sanctus, Agnus Dei and the Benedictus. The Mass Proper consisted of the various activities necessary to supplement the Mass Ordinary, depending on the emphasis of the day. Other kinds of Masses for special occasions also were developed during this time. These included High Mass, Solemn High Mass, Low Mass, Requiem Mass of the Pre-sanctified, Nuptial Mass, Votive Mass. The liturgy of these Masses is important since it has provided the musical structures for many of the finest choral compositions by master composers of both Catholic and Protestant faiths for many centuries. An example is Bach's B Minor Mass.

This medieval period also witnessed the growth of harmony, progressing from unison singing to the harmonizing of two or more voices to a main melody voice. These main melody parts, known as the *cantus firmus*, were generally borrowed from the earlier church chants. The complicated polyphonic and contrapuntal devices used in this music reached their complete fruition in the music of two of the finest composers of sacred music of all time, Palestrina of the sixteenth century and J. S. Bach, 1685-1750. Other important musical developments from approximately 1150 to 1450, generally referred to as the Gothic Period during the Middle Ages, included the use of antiphonal singing; the development of the staff and the system of modern notation; and the rise of the instrumental concept, especially with regard to the use of church organs.

IV. THE RENAISSANCE-REFORMATION PERIOD

The next period of time of historical importance is the Renaissance-Reformation Period from approximately 1450 to 1600. This period marked a great revival of interest in intellectual activity and in the arts. In the religious sense, the Reformation, which was climaxed by Martin Luther with his Ninety-five Theses at the Augsburg Confession in 1517, was extremely important both theologically and musically to all followers of this new movement. Once again the barrier of an intermediary priesthood between the believer and his God was broken down. Much of that same joy known by the early Christians during the apostolic period was again experienced by the Christians of the Reformation as they realized anew the truths of a personal relationship with God through faith in Jesus Christ alone.

It was perfectly natural that with this new found personal joy there came the desire to express adoration and praise in one's own vernacular language. Congregational singing of hymns and chorales was a powerful force in this new movement. Both friends and foes of Luther often said that he gained more converts through his use and encouragement of congregational singing than he did through his preaching. Luther himself said that music was one of the finest and noblest gifts of God in the world and that young men should not be ordained as preachers unless they had also been trained in music.

Other important reformers of this period such as John Calvin and Ulrich Zwingli also realized the importance of congregational singing, although not with the same intensity that Luther did. Calvin, while insisting that the ear should not be more attentive to the harmony of sounds than the soul to the hidden meanings of the words, did decree in Geneva that music should be taught to the children in the day school, so that when they had learned to sing the Psalms thoroughly there, they might sing properly in the public worship services on Sundays. Since these reformers felt that only songs with Scriptural settings were proper for worship, only the metrical versions of the Psalms were used in churches of Reformed conviction, and then sung only in unison. Clement Marot was one of the Reformed Church musicians most responsible for various publications of metrical psalmody during this time. The most important psalter was the *Geneva Psalter*, published in 1562. The musician who supplied most of the tunes for this psalter was Louis Bourgeois. Another important psalter of this time was the *Scottish Psalter*, published in Scotland in 1564.

The Reformation in England was quite different from that upon the continent. In Germany, France, Switzerland and the Netherlands the revolt against Rome was primarily religious. In England, the break with Rome was not because of doctrinal disagreement, but solely for political advantage. In 1534, Henry VIII issued a royal edict repudiating the papal authority. Although this accomplished a separation with Rome, there were no basic changes in the doctrines of the Church of England. Edward VI, 1547-1553, was much more receptive to the true spirit of the Reformation as England more and more felt its influence from the other countries. During Edward's reign, two religious leaders, Thomas Sternhold and John Hopkins, were influential in making several important publications available to the English public. The *Book of Common Prayer*, containing the entire ritual of the Anglican Church, was published in 1549 while the complete setting of metrical psalmody was published in 1562. During the reign of "Bloody" Mary, 1553-1558, there was a brief return to Catholicism in England. However, with the rule of Elizabeth, 1558-1603, Protestantism was once again permanently restored. One of the important injunctions issued by Queen Elizabeth was in 1559 when she declared: "In the beginning, or at the end of Common Prayer, there may be sung a hymn or such like song to the praise of Almighty God, in the best sort of melody and music that may be conveniently devised." With that encouragement came the gradual rise of English hymnody, with its rich treasures of poetry and music.

V. THE SEVENTEENTH CENTURY

Among the most bitter opponents of the Anglican Church during this time were the Puritans. They repeatedly assailed the church as being half-papist. They did their best to reduce worship to the barest simplicity as well as to set up a more democratic form of church government. Their influence was first exerted during the time of Queen Elizabeth, but as a result of her strong stand for the established church, they were repressed. The Puritan movement increased in fervor under the weaker rule of James I, 1603-1625, and finally culminated with the overthrow of the monarchy during the reign of Charles I, 1625-1649. This temporary triumph was completed with the rule of the Commonwealth replacing that of the monarchy from 1649-1660. With the restoration of the throne in 1660, the liturgy and elaborate musical service of the Church of England were re-established.

The non-ceremonial practices of the Puritans were largely promoted by the fervent teachings of John Calvin on the continent. As is often the case, however, the followers were far more extreme in their practices than was their leader. Though the Puritans gave strict adherence to such Calvinistic ideals as complete acceptance of the Scriptures for all rule and authority of life, the acceptance of only the metrical psalms sung in unison for congregational singing, refusal to accept choirs and church organs, their ruthless and radical tactics for accomplishing these ideals will always be one of the dark blights in church history. As the Puritans reacted to the High Church, many ancient sanctuaries were demolished, stained glass windows broken, ornaments torn down, libraries ransacked, and many fine church organs completely destroyed by this religious fanaticism.

With the restoration of the Stuart rule, Charles II, 1660-1685, and the re-establishment of the Anglican Church liturgy, there developed an important new musical form, the anthem. The ancient antiphonal form of the anthem was actually the counterpart of the choral motet of the Catholic Mass. The modern form of the anthem in the English language is attributed to the influence of one of England's finest composers, Henry Purcell, 1658-1695. The anthem in its present form is a mixture of the ancient motet and the German cantata. The modern anthems are generally found in three forms: The full anthem, where all voices are used throughout; the verse anthem, where portions are sung by selected voices; and the solo anthem, containing passages for a single voice.

During the seventeenth century other minority groups continued to rebel against the established church. These groups were known as Dissenters or Non-Conformists. After their first wave of initial enthusiasm wore off, things went progressively worse for these groups. The dullness and plainness of their services as well as their fantastic concepts of individualism, which led many of the leaders to expound the idea that singing as well as praying should be completely spontaneous in a service, nearly led to the ruin of sacred music in these churches.

VI. THE EIGHTEENTH CENTURY

The eighteenth century truly was ready for the new hymns of Isaac Watts, 1674-1748, often called the "father of English hymnody," and the soul stirring music of the Wesleys. The myth of "inspired psalmody" was soon shattered as Christians everywhere thrilled in singing this new type of sacred music. As was said of the Lutheran chorales, so it can be said of these hymns: They often were more instrumental in winning converts to Christ than was the preaching of the leading evangelists of this time, John Wesley, 1703-1791, and George Whitefield, 1714-1770.

Isaac Watts used his hymns to summarize his sermons and to express his Calvinistic theology. He firmly believed that since songs are human offerings of praise to God, the words, therefore, ought to be one's own. If the Psalms were to be used, he contended that they ought to be Christianized and modernized. Being a Dissenter and Congregationalist and having the convictions that he did, Watts was often called a revolutionist in his day. Several of his best known hymns found in our hymnals today are "When I Survey the Wondrous Cross"; "Jesus Shall Reign Wher'er the Sun"; "Joy to the World"; "O God, Our Help in Ages Past"; "Before Jehovah's Awful Throne."

The Wesleyan Movement was the spark that set off a great revival of religious fervor. This did much to combat the spirit of agnosticism that was so prevalent during this time. The state churches had become more and more corrupt, with little concern for the individual. Even the dissenting groups were becoming easy-going and non-evangelistic. The new vitalized singing introduced by the Wesleys was an important factor in these great revivals. Together, John the preacher and Charles the musician (1708-1788) wrote and translated approximately 6,500 hymns, although the majority are no longer found in our hymnals today. Their theology was strongly opposed to the "election" emphasis of Calvin's teachings. They wrote hymns on nearly every phase of Christian experience with warmth and conviction. Several of their best known hymns found in our hymnals today are "Jesus, Lover of My Soul"; "Love Divine, All Loves Excelling"; "O For a Thousand Tongues to Sing"; "Soldiers of Christ, Arise"; "Ye Servants of God, Your Master Proclaim"; "Hark! the Herald Angels Sing"; "Christ the Lord Is Risen Today."

In addition to the names of Watts and Wesley, the eighteenth century also produced other well-known hymn composers such as Joseph Addison, 1672-1719, "When All Thy Mercies, O My God"; Philip Doddridge, 1702-1751, "O Happy Day That Fixed My Choice"; Anne Steele, 1716-1778, "Father of Mercies, in Thy Word"; Joseph Grigg, 1720-1768, "Jesus, and Shall It Ever Be"; William Williams, 1717-1781, "Guide Me, O Thou Great Jehovah"; John Cennick, 1718-1755, "Children of the Heavenly King"; John Byrom, 1692-1763, "Christians, Awake, Salute the Happy Morn"; Thomas Olivers, 1725-1799, "The God of Abraham Praise"; Augustus Toplady, 1740-1778, "Rock of Ages, Cleft for Me"; Edward Perronet, 1721-1792, "All Hail the Power of Jesus' Name"; John Newton, 1725-1807, "Amazing Grace, How Sweet the Sound"; William Cowper, 1731-1800, "God Moves in a Mysterious Way"; John Fawcett, 1739-1817, "Blest Be the Tie That Binds"; George Heath, 1745-1822, "My Soul, Be on Thy Guard." Other well-known eighteenth century hymns whose authors are unknown are: "Come, Thou Almighty King," "How Firm a Foundation," and "Praise the Lord! Ye Heavens Adore Him."

The eighteenth century also produced another important form of sacred music, the oratorio. Although Germany's Heinrich Schutz, 1585-1672, and still later J. S. Bach, 1685-1750, had written much fine dramatic music known as Passion Music, which presented texts based on the sufferings of Christ as recorded in the various gospels,

George Frederick Handel, 1685-1759, was one of the first to write sacred dramatic music in the English language. His most popular oratorio, *The Messiah,* was first performed in Ireland in 1742. Other later important oratorio composers were: Franz Joseph Haydn, 1732-1809, *The Creation;* Felix Mendelssohn, 1809-1847, *The Elijah.*

VII. The Nineteenth Century

Whereas most of the hymn writers of the seventeenth and eighteenth centuries were primarily concerned with composing hymns that expressed a particular emphasis of their doctrinal convictions, nineteenth century hymnists, influenced by the prevailing Romantic Age spirit found in all forms of art, were more concerned with improving the literary quality of hymnody. Important hymn composers of this time included Reginald Heber, 1783-1826, "Holy, Holy, Holy"; Thomas Kelly, 1769-1854, "Look, Ye Saints, the Sight Is Glorious"; Thomas Moore, 1779-1852, "Come, Ye Disconsolate"; James Montgomery, 1771-1854, "In the Hour of Trial"; John Keble, 1792-1866, "Sun of My Soul"; James Edmeston, 1791-1867, "Savior, Breathe an Evening Blessing"; Henry Hart Milman, 1791-1868, "Ride On! Ride On in Majesty"; Henry Francis Lyte, 1793-1847, "Abide With Me"; Sir John Bowring, 1792-1872, "In the Cross of Christ I Glory"; Hugh Stowel, 1799-1865, "From Every Stormy Wind That Blows"; Andrew Reed, 1787-1862, "Holy Ghost, With Light Divine"; William Hiley Bathurst, 1796-1877, "O For a Faith That Will Not Shrink"; Sir Robert Grant, 1779-1838, "O Worship the King"; Charlotte Elliott, 1789-1871, "Just As I Am." Another fine hymn of this time, which remains anonymous, is "Savior, Like a Shepherd Lead Us."

On July 14, 1833, a new religious movement in England known as the Oxford or Tractarian Movement was begun with a sermon by John Keble entitled "National Apostasy." This movement was originally intended to vindicate the privileges of the state church under the threat of spoilation by a Whig government by defending the theory of a Catholic and Apostolic Church ordained by Christ Himself. It also sought to establish a more devout and reverent worship with a renewed use of music in the service. This emphasis was a reaction to much of the indifferent and careless worship of that time. For ten years this movement held religious England with great tenacity, during which time many of the church's leaders either went back to the Roman Church or became a rejuvenated High Church Party known as Anglo-Catholics. This influence was also felt in many other Protestant churches with such practices as the institution of boys' choirs, the use of vestments, and other elaborate ritualistic practices such as the use of symbols, processionals and recessionals. Important hymn writers who were influenced by this movement were John Henry Newman, 1801-1890, "Lead, Kindly Light"; Edward Caswall, 1814-1878, "When Morning Gilds the Skies"; John Mason Neale, 1818-1866, "The Day of Resurrection." Both Caswall and Neale are primarily noted for their work in translating some of the Greek and Latin hymns of the early church fathers. Other church leaders such as Frederick William Faber, 1814-1863, "Faith of Our Fathers, Living Still," and Matthew Bridges, 1800-1894, "Crown Him With Many Crowns," later became prominent leaders in the Roman Catholic Church. In 1861 this movement produced an important hymnal, *Hymns Ancient and Modern*, for High Church use.

At the height of the Oxford Movement, Queen Victoria, who ruled England from 1837-1901, inherited the throne. The hymns written throughout this Victorian Era are generally classified as being High Church Hymns; Evangelical or Low Church Hymns; Broad Church Hymns; Dissenting Hymns; Post-Victorian Hymns.

A. *High Church Hymn Writers of the Victorian Era.* These churchmen were Anglicans who resisted the drift toward Rome as well as toward the spirit of agnosticism, which was prevalent at this time. They were primarily concerned with preserving the integrity of the liturgy, creeds, sacraments and practices of the Anglican Church. Important hymn composers of this group included: Mrs. Cecil Frances Alexander, 1818-1895, "There Is a Green Hill Far Away"; Christopher Wordsworth, 1807-1885, "O Day of Rest and Gladness"; William Whiting, 1825-1878, "Eternal Father, Strong to Save"; Francis Pott, 1832-1909, "Angel Voices Ever Singing"; Folliett Sandford Pierpoint, 1835-1917, "For the Beauty of the Earth"; Edward Hayes Plumptre, 1821-1891, "Rejoice, Ye Pure in Heart"; Sabine Baring-Gould, 1834-1924, "Onward, Christian Soldiers"; Samuel John Stone, 1839-1900, "The Church's One Foundation"; and Dorothy Frances Gurney, 1858-1932, "O Perfect Love, All Human Thought Transcending."

B. *The Evangelical or Low Church Hymn Writers of the Victorian Era.* These churchmen were Anglicans who also remained in the Anglican Church but who were generally more concerned with the spiritual and social welfare of individuals rather than in merely maintaining the integrity and practices of the church. Important hymn composers of this group included: Anna Laetitia Waring, 1820-1910, "In Heavenly Love Abiding"; Dean

Henry Alford, 1810-1871, "Come, Ye Thankful People, Come"; George Croly, 1780-1860, "Spirit of God, Descend Upon My Heart"; Emily Elizabeth Steele Elliott, 1836-1897, "Thou Didst Leave Thy Throne and Thy Kingly Crown"; Arabella Katherine Hankey, 1834-1889, "I Love to Tell the Story"; Frances Ridley Havergal, 1836-1878, "Take My Life and Let It Be."

C. *Broad Church Hymn Writers of the Victorian Era.* This group of churchmen represented the liberal and modern faction in the Anglican Church. They supported the traditions and practices of the established church but attempted to reconcile the church with higher criticism and scientific and philosophical findings and developments. Important hymn composers of this group included Alfred Lord Tennyson, 1809-1892, "Strong Son of God, Immortal Love"; William Walsham How, 1823-1897, "O Word of God Incarnate"; John Ellerton, 1826-1893, "Savior, Again to Thy Dear Name We Raise"; John Ernest Bode, 1816-1874, "O Jesus, I Have Promised"; Edwin Hatch, 1835-1889, "Breathe On Me, Breath of God"; Rudyard Kipling, 1865-1936, "Father in Heaven, Who Lovest All."

D. *Dissenting Church Hymn Writers of the Victorian Era.* This group represented those who had broken from the established state churches in England or Scotland. The greatest number of these independent writers were of Scotch Presbyterian background. Important hymn composers of this group included: Horatius Bonar, 1808-1889, "I Heard the Voice of Jesus Say"; Elizabeth Douglas Clephane, 1830-1869, "Beneath the Cross of Jesus"; George Matheson, 1842-1906, "O Love That Wilt Not Let Me Go"; Sarah Flower Adams, 1805-1848, "Nearer, My God, to Thee"; Thomas Toke Lynch, 1818-1871, "Gracious Spirit, Dwell With Me."

E. *Post-Victorian Church Hymn Writers.* The following English hymn writers have written important hymns following the death of Queen Victoria in 1901 and throughout the reigns of Edward VII (1901-1910), George V (1910-1936), George VI (1936-1952), and Queen Elizabeth (1952-   ). Several of these composers are: John Oxenham, 185?-1941, "In Christ There Is No East or West"; Frank Fletcher, 1870-1936, "O Son of Man, Our Hero Strong and Tender"; Clifford Bax, 1886-   , "Turn Back, O Man, Forswear Thy Foolish Ways."

F *Russian Choral Music.* Another important contribution to the field of sacred music was made in the latter half of the nineteenth century by a group of Russian composers. This choral music, with its intensely emotional and worshipful character, modal harmonies and extreme ranges, is an outgrowth of the Greek Orthodox Church, which had separated from the Western Roman Church in 1054 A.D. The many fine "cherubim songs" and other anthems of praise written in this style are used in worship services in many of our evangelical churches. Several of these leading Russian composers are: Michael Glinka, 1804-1857; Dimitri Bortniansky, 1751-1825; Mili Balakirev, 1837-1910; César Cui, 1835-1918; Alexander Borodin, 1834-1887; Rimsky Korsakoff, 1844-1908; Modeste Moussorgsky, 1835-1881; Peter Tchaikovsky, 1840-1893.

VIII. Sacred Music in America

In America, the early settlers used the psalters taught them in England, still clinging to the idea that God would be insulted if men offered to Him any hymns other than those He had dictated in Scripture. The Puritans of Salem used the *Sternhold* and *Hopkins Psalter*, while the Pilgrims at Plymouth brought the *Ainsworth Psalter*, and later made their own metrical version, the *Bay Psalm Book*, published in 1640. In the eighteenth century and early part of the nineteenth century, the "human composure" hymns of Watts, Wesley, and other English hymn writers gradually became accepted in American churches. It is interesting to note that during our early history, 1620-1820, only one hymn from the pen of an American composer is still found in our hymnals today. This hymn, "I Love Thy Kingdom, Lord," written by Timothy Dwight, 1752-1817, influential in education, theology and literature, is still widely sung.

Perhaps the most distinct form of sacred music contributed to hymnology by the Americans is the gospel song. This has been defined and described by Edmund S. Lorenz in his book, *Church Music: What a Minister Should Know About It*, as follows: "A sacred folk song, free in form, emotional in character, devout in attitude, evangelistic in purpose and spirit. The hymns are more or less subjective in their matter and develop a single thought, rather than a line of thought. That thought usually finds its supreme expression in the chorus or refrain which binds the stanzas together in a very close unity, just as it does in lyrical poetry where it is occasionally used."[1]

The gospel song is generally said to have had its outgrowth from the spirituals and early Sunday school songs of the nineteenth century. The gospel songs received their real impetus, however, in

---

[1]Edmund Simon Lorenz, *Church Music: What a Minister Should Know About It* (New York: Fleming H. Revell Co., 1923), p. 342.

the latter part of the nineteenth century with the evangelistic endeavors of D. L. Moody and Ira Sankey, both in this country and in Great Britain. Once again, as had been experienced by the apostolic church Christians, by the Christians of the Reformation period, and by the Christians who sang the hymns of Watts and Wesley, people rediscovered the thrill of raising their voices in praise and thanksgiving to God. These were songs which had a melody and rhythm easy to sing as well as words that were easy to understand. The words expressed truths that had warmth and personal meaning to those who sang them. These are the songs that have characterized the singing in many of our evangelical churches to the present time.

IX. IMPORTANT GOSPEL SONG WRITERS

Some of the earliest important gospel song writers include: Charles H. Gabriel, E. O. Excell, P. P. Bliss, Fanny Crosby, William Bradbury, Robert Lowry, James McGranahan, George Stebbins, William Doane, C. C. Converse, James M. Gray, A. H. Ackley, B. D. Ackley, H. Lillenas, Wm. J. Kirkpatrick, W. A. Ogden, C. Austin Miles, A. T. Pierson, Charles Alexander, and Homer Rodeheaver.

Several of the present day gospel song writers include: Beatrice Bixler, Norman Clayton, Merrill Dunlop, Robert Harkness, Robert J. Hughes, Paul Hutchens, Phil Kerr, Harry Dixon Loes, Wendell P. Loveless, John Peterson, George Schuler, Al Smith, Herman Voss, Keith Whitford. It should be noted that many of the musical changes taking place in contemporary secular serious music are also found to some degree in present day gospel songs and anthems. These musical changes include: More emphasis on dissonant harmonies, more rhythmic variety, and more emotional restraint. Several of the leading contemporary composers writing sacred anthems in this modern style include: Randall Thompson, Gustav Holst, and Ralph Vaughan Williams.

X. AMERICAN HYMN WRITERS OF THE NINETEENTH AND TWENTIETH CENTURIES

In addition to the name of Timothy Dwight, other important American hymn writers are: Thomas Hastings, 1784-1872, "Hail to the Brightness of Zion's Glad Morning"; George Doane, 1799-1859, "Fling Out the Banner!"; Ray Palmer, 1808-1887, "My Faith Looks Up to Thee"; Samuel Francis Smith, 1808-1895, "My Country, 'Tis of Thee"; Joseph Scriven, 1820-1886, "What a Friend We Have in

Jesus"; Harriet Beecher Stowe, 1811-1896, "Still, Still With Thee, When Purple Morning Breaketh"; Elizabeth Payson Prentiss, 1818-1878, "More Love to Thee, O Christ"; George Duffield, 1818-1888, "Stand Up, Stand Up For Jesus"; Edmund Hamilton Sears, 1810-1876, "It Came Upon the Midnight Clear"; Sylvanus Dryden Phelps, 1816-1895, "Savior, Thy Dying Love"; John Henry Gilmore, 1834-1918, "He Leadeth Me! O Blessed Thought"; Mary Ann Thomson, 1834-1923, "O Zion, Haste"; Edward Hopper, 1816-1888, "Jesus, Savior, Pilot Me"; Annie Sherwood Hawks, 1835-1918, "I Need Thee Every Hour"; Daniel Crane Roberts, 1841-1907, "God of Our Fathers, Whose Mighty Hand"; Mary Artemesia Lathbury, 1841-1918, "Break Thou the Bread of Life"; Jeremiah Eames Rankin, 1828-1904, "God Be With You Till We Meet Again"; John Greenleaf Whittier, 1807-1892, "Dear Lord and Father of Mankind"; Phillips Brooks, 1853-1893, "O Little Town of Bethlehem"; Ernest Warburton Shurtleff, 1862-1917, "Lead On, O King Eternal"; Maltbie Davenport Babcock, 1858-1901, "This Is My Father's World"; Henry Van Dyke, 1852-1933, "Joyful, Joyful, We Adore Thee"; Washington Gladden, 1838-1918, "O Master, Let Me Walk With Thee."

It can generally be said that hymn writers of the late nineteenth and the twentieth centuries, both in this country and in England, were more concerned with writing texts that expressed the virtues, ethics and social implications of the Gospel rather than in expounding doctrinal truths.

XI. A LOOK AT THE PAST, PRESENT AND FUTURE

A study of the past reveals that the Christian church has inherited rich musical treasures throughout the centuries from such sources as: translations of Greek and Latin hymns; hymns and chorales from the Reformation period; metrical psalmody embodied in Calvin, Marot, and psalters of this time; the free verse, "human composure" hymns of Watts, Wesley and other seventeenth and eighteenth century composers with their strong doctrinal teachings; the fine literary hymns of the early nineteenth century; the gospel music of the nineteenth and twentieth centuries, especially useful for evangelistic endeavors; and the late nineteenth and twentieth century hymns with their greater emphasis on Christian behavior and the social responsibilities of the Gospel. A good church hymnal should be representative of all of these sources of hymnody.

A look at the present and future indicates many favorable trends taking place in evangelical church music. More Bible schools, colleges and seminaries are giving emphasis and instruction in church music than ever before.

Another promising sign for church music is the greater interest shown by many church leaders. This is indicated in the growing number of church music conferences, clinics, and workshops held periodically around the country. It is also encouraging to note that more churches, both large and small, are beginning to see the value of having more than just a senior choir. These churches realize that if there is to be a good senior choir in the future, it must begin with the children and carry through each age group. Further, since the music and education ministries are closely related, a total music program in a church serves as an important tool in developing a strong Christian education program. The fact remains, however, that there is yet much to be accomplished. The great majority of evangelical churches still do not have a music ministry that has a vital influence on its individual members.

XII. CONCLUSION

Any church music director soon realizes that achieving an effective and total music program in an individual church is usually a slow, tedious task, requiring much effort and patience. There generally are such factors as indifference, complacency, deficient musical education, traditions and prejudices that must be overcome. It is quite possible that a music director may never see the fruition of his work during his own ministry in a church. However, one must continually remind himself that a Christian leader should be interested primarily in faithfulness to God and the ideals of the future rather than self-glory and mere apparent success.

Although there is a continual struggle on the part of church music directors for better musical standards, it should be cautioned that good music and a large music program are not merely ends in themselves. The ultimate objectives of the church music program must always be to attract individuals to a saving knowledge of Jesus Christ and then to lead them to a fuller, more Spirit-filled Christian life. This is the ministry of music with which we must be earnestly concerned.

ASSIGNMENTS

1. In what ways can an understanding of the historical development of sacred music be helpful to a church music director?
2. Discuss the importance of music to the Hebrews as recorded throughout the Old Testament. Discuss the basic differences between Hebrew worship and Christian worship of the apostolic period. Discuss the history, meaning, structure and musical importance of the Mass.
3. Discuss why the Reformation as climaxed by Martin Luther in 1517 is important both theologically and musically to the evangelical church.
4. Discuss the differences between the hymns of the seventeenth and eighteenth centuries and the hymns of the nineteenth and twentieth centuries.
5. Discuss ways and means of improving the total music program in the local evangelical church.

ADDITIONAL READING

1. *Christian Music in Contemporary Witness* by Donald Ellsworth. Published by Baker Book House.
2. *Church Music in History and Practice* by Douglas. Published by C. Scribner's Sons.
3. *Church Music: What a Minister Should Know About It* by Edmund S. Lorenz. Published by Fleming H. Revell Co.
4. *Jubilate! Church Music in The Evangelical Tradition* by Donald Hustad. Published by Hope Publishing Co.
5. *Patterns of Protestant Church Music* by Stevenson. Published by Duke University Press.
6. *Protestant Church Music in America* by Davison. Published by E. C. Schirmer Co.
7. *The Gospel in Hymns* by Bailey. Published by Charles Scribner's Sons.
8. *The Hymnody of the Christian Church* by Benson. Published by George H. Doran Co.
9. *The Rise and Growth of English Hynmody* by Marks. Published by Fleming H. Revell Co.
10. *The Story of Our Hymns* by Halussler. Published by Eden Publishing Co.

2 | QUALIFICATIONS OF A CHURCH MUSIC DIRECTOR

If a church is to have an effective and total music program, it must first of all have a congregation, a church board, a pastor and music committee that are sympathetic and appreciative of the music ministry. Such a church then faces the often difficult task of finding the right type of leader to administer this program. In some churches this person is known as the Music Director; in other churches, The Minister of Music. In some churches this work is done in combination with other forms of service such as: Assistant Pastor and Music Director; Youth Director and Music Director; or Parish Worker and Music Director. It is not too uncommon in many smaller churches for the pastor or his wife to lead these activities; in some cases the work is divided among several lay or part-time directors with the pastor or music committee responsible for overseeing the total program. It is vitally important, therefore, that anyone preparing for any form of Christian leadership have a basic knowledge of music and a vision of the total church music program.

A church music director must be qualified in three main areas: the spiritual, the personal, the musical. Each of these areas will be considered in this chapter.

I. Spiritual

There are churches that will engage a music director simply for his musical abilities, with little or no regard for his spiritual life. Basic, then, is the fact that any church music leader must first of all be a real Christian, one with a living relationship with God through a personal faith in the person and redemptive work of Jesus Christ. Such a person must have a life that is known and respected by all of his associates for its positive Christian witness.

Further, this type of Christian leader must have clearly defined convictions and goals that govern and color all of his work. He must feel as strongly called of God and as consecrated for this type of service as is the one who ministers the spoken Word. He must believe that his job is that of ministering spiritually to others, not that of displaying his own talents or of providing mere entertainment for people. He must have confidence in the fact that music does have a unique way of ministering to people's spiritual needs when it is presented with the power of the Holy Spirit. A music director must also feel his work to be a sacred trust, realizing that music has as much potential for evil purposes when it is debased and the product of the flesh as it can have for good when it is Spirit directed.

II. PERSONAL

Since human leadership is largely a matter of personality, the sum and substance of all that is in a person, a music director must consciously strive to develop a wholesome personality. His life should give evidence of an inner fortitude as well as the outgoing warmth of a mature, stable person. The spiritual standard of personality is found in Galatians 5:22, 23: "But the fruit of the Spirit is love, joy, peace, longsuffering, gentleness, goodness, faith, meekness, temperance: against such there is no law." Paramount traits of a Christian leader, then, are sincerity and humility. There is no place in Christian service for the musical leader who sets himself above the rest of the group, or for the one who desires the job simply for the authority he can exert over others. Further, a music director must thoroughly love people of all ages. He must develop a genuine friendship with each individual in his various groups. A director must learn to sensitize himself to each personality so that he can deal positively with it. This means that the director must have a fundamentally warm and sympathetic personality.

In brief, other traits that should characterize a Christian music leader are: a neat, well-groomed appearance; an enthusiastic attitude; organizational and promotional ability; aggressiveness; humor; persistence; tact; the ability to inspire others. In general, a music director's entire personality, character, appearance, knowledge and poise must naturally command respect from those he leads. Needless to say, no one is imbued with all of these attributes. In fact, it must be admitted that there are few "natural born" music leaders. However, it is possible through study, application and the help of the Holy Spirit for one to develop the qualities essential for success as a director.

Not only must a music director learn to lead his own musical organizations, but he must also learn the art of working with and under other leaders in the church. He must learn that he cannot always expect to have his own way and must recognize that the church board, pastor and music committee represent higher authority. He must learn to work in harmony with these people despite "how wrong" they might be. It is a tragic fact that there has been a great deal of church difficulty simply because leaders (and music directors in particular) have never learned what it means to compromise if need be on personal differences in order to maintain a spirit of unity in the work of the Lord. It has well been said that the test of a good leader is not how strongly he can push his plans forward, but how effectively he can accomplish his purposes and still retain the co-operation and support of his associates.

III. MUSICAL

Assuming that a person has the necessary innate musical ability, there are still various musical areas in which he will need development and training. A director must have a factual and thorough grasp of the fundamentals of music used in the system of notation. This would include a knowledge of the following:

A. *Fundamentals*

    1. Position and names of the notes on the staffs:

Middle C

    2. Note values and their relationships:

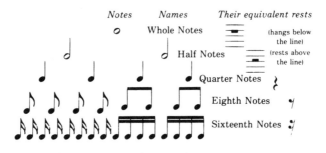

A dot after a note adds one-half of the time value of the note it follows.

Example

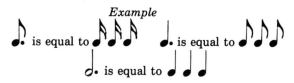

3. Time Signatures:

a. The top number states the number of beats to a measure.

b. The bottom number identifies the kind of note that gets a beat:

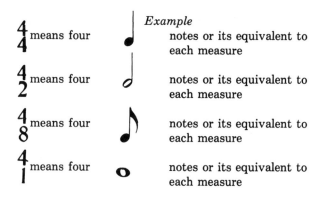

c. Compound Rhythms when the top number of the time signature is either 6, 9, or 12, the music may be performed in one of two ways: Either in the total number of beats as indicated by the top number generally for a slow song, or in a more "lilting" rhythm achieved by singing the notes indicated by the bottom number in groups of threes.

Example

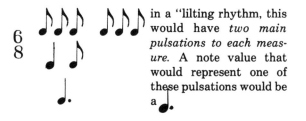

in a "lilting rhythm, this would have *two main pulsations to each measure*. A note value that would represent one of these pulsations would be a

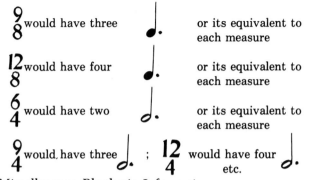

$\frac{9}{8}$ would have three ♩.   or its equivalent to each measure

$\frac{12}{8}$ would have four ♩.   or its equivalent to each measure

$\frac{6}{4}$ would have two ♩.   or its equivalent to each measure

$\frac{9}{4}$ would have three ♩. ; $\frac{12}{4}$ would have four ♩. etc.

d. Miscellaneous Rhythmic Information:

The first beat of a measure is the strong or accented beat.

𝄴 refers to common or 4/4 time signature. This symbol is often used in place of the numerical figures.

𝄵 refers to a "cut" 4/4 rhythm or singing the music with two beats to a measure. The 𝅗𝅥 note instead of the ♩ note now becomes the unit of beat.

4. Key Signatures as indicated by the number of sharps (♯) or flats (♭) after the clef sign.

a. A sharp raises a note ½ step. A double sharp (𝄪) raises a note a whole step.

b. A flat lowers a note ½ step. A double flat (♭♭) lowers a note a whole step.

c. A natural (♮) destroys the previous effect of either a flat or sharp for the remainder of that measure.

Key Names

No flats or sharps ..... Key C

1 ♯ ....Key G	4 ♭'s ..Key A♭
1 ♭ ....Key F	5 ♯'s...Key B
2 ♯'s...Key D	5 ♭'s ..Key D♭
2 ♭'s...Key B♭	6 ♯'s...Key F♯
3 ♯'s...Key A	6 ♭'s ..Key G♭
3 ♭'s...Key E♭	7 ♯'s...Key C♯
4 ♯'s...Key E	7 ♭'s...Key C♭

d. These key signature names refer to songs that have a major sound. When a song has one of these signatures but has a minor sound, it is said to be the related minor key of that particular key signature. The minor key is always pitched 1½ steps lower than its major key signature. Example—*the key of a minor* has no flats or sharps and is 1½ *steps lower* than the *key of C*.

In addition to a factual grasp of the fundamentals of music, a director should have a strong rhythmic sense, the ability to maintain a definite, steady beat, as well as the ability to sing any rhythmic pattern quickly and accurately. A director must also develop the ability to sight read any voice part easily. A director needs an infallible musical ear so that he is keenly sensitive to pitch. This musical ear should also help him to hear music mentally. For all of these developments a working knowledge of the piano is almost a necessity for any music director. A director must develop an awareness of the emotional meanings and moods of texts, as well as a realization of the union or lack of union between the music and the text. A director's creative abilities need to be challenged and developed. When examining a printed page of music, a good director is able to foresee the possibility of transforming mere notes and words into messages of beauty and blessing. He has to have imagination and creative ability for planning special programs, devising ways of maintaining interest in his groups, and, if at all possible, the ability to make his own musical arrangements and compositions when necessary. A music director should have a knowledge of the terms and expressions frequently used in music. A music director should also have an appreciation and understanding of the term "style" in music — a realization that each song must be interpreted in the manner that is appropriate for that number. This would imply a basic acquaintance with music history and literature, as well as with the study of hymnology.

A church music director must be trained in spiritual and musical discernment for choosing appropriate music for each type of service or program. For example, music that is suitable for an evangelistic or gospel service is generally not suited for a worship service. Music that is suited for a youth or Sunday school meeting is quite likely inappropriate for the prayer service, etc.

B. *Different Types of Sacred Song.* A music director should, then, be acquainted with the main types of sacred literature and should have discernment in the proper usage of each. It should be added, however, that the final criterion for the choice of any number in an evangelical church should always be that the song to be used is one that best presents a particular truth of the gospel message in the most effective manner to the greatest number of people. The following are brief descriptions of the different types of sacred music:

1. Hymns. Expressions of praise, adoration, worship, confes-

sion, vows of service, etc., that are addressed to God with a sense of reverence and dignity to the music as well as to the words. These songs are essentially objective or God-centered in character. They are best used for worship services.

2. Gospel Songs or Gospel Hymns. Musical expressions that speak of one's personal experience with the Lord; or that are spiritual exhortations to other Christians; or that present an invitation to the non-Christian to accept Christ as Saviour. The words are essentially subjective or man-centered in character. The music, too, has more rhythmic emphasis than does the hymn. These songs are excellent for evangelistic meetings or for devotional purposes.

3. Hymn or Gospel Song Arrangements. Familiar hymns or gospel songs especially arranged with some form of musical variation to make for greater listening interest and to enhance the meaning of the words. These songs can be used by a choir for either worship or evangelistic services, depending on the character of the song and the type of arrangement.

4. Choruses. Short, direct, gospel truths generally set to lyrical tunes and emphasized rhythms. These songs are best used for gospel meetings, youth meetings, and Sunday school services.

5. Anthems. More complex choral compositions with texts taken quite directly from the Scriptures. These songs generally employ considerable repetition, which is done for the purpose of achieving emphasis. These songs are excellent for a choir to use for a worship service.

6. Chorales. Stately hymns that began with the time of Martin Luther and the Reformation. Examples: "A Mighty Fortress"; "Doxology." These songs are best used for a worship service.

7. Psalms. Words either taken directly or paraphrased from the Book of Psalms and set to stately music. These songs are best used for a worship service.

8. Motets. Lengthy, complex choral compositions written in a contrapuntal style (each voice part an independent melody in itself). These songs are best used for special programs or concerts.

9. Oratorios. Lengthy, dramatic compositions for solo voices and choir, with orchestral accompaniment if possible (otherwise organ). These works depict Biblical stories or scenes without employing acting or scenery. Examples: *The Messiah, The Elijah, The Creation, St. Paul,* etc. These are works that a choir can perform for special occasions. It is also possible to use individual numbers from these works for regular worship services.

10. Cantata. A shorter form of oratorio, consisting of various

movements such as solos, duets, choir, etc., all of which are based on a continuous narrative text. This music is especially good for a choir to perform at special seasons of the year, such as Christmas and Easter.

From these available sources, a music director should try as often as possible to choose appropriate music that complements a pastor's message or a special emphasis a church may have for a particular service. Most churches have periodic services with such emphasis as: special holidays, missionary endeavors, dedicatory services, communion services, Reformation Day services, Christian Education Day, etc. Some churches follow more closely the plan of the church calendar, which is the organization of the events of Christ's life into a yearly schedule. This church year calendar plan is as follows:

Advent — begins the fourth Sunday preceding Christmas Eve. The emphasis is the Messianic prophecies concerning the birth of Christ. The church color for this season is purple.

Christmas Time — begins with Christmas Eve and extends for twelve nights to January fifth. The emphasis is on the birth of Christ. The church color for this season is white.

Epiphany — this period begins with January sixth and extends to Ash Wednesday, or the Wednesday before the sixth Sunday preceding Easter. The emphasis is that of the Christ Child being revealed to the wise men and is symbolic of the revealing of Himself to all Gentiles as the Light of the world. Usually this period is ushered in with a special week of prayer. It is also a time for a church missionary emphasis. The church color for this season is green.

Lent — begins with Ash Wednesday and includes forty weekdays and six Sundays preceding Easter. The emphasis is that of spiritual self-examination and rededicated living. The church color for this season is purple. The church color for the Good Friday service is black.

Eastertide — begins with Easter Sunday and extends for fifty days, including Ascension Day, and for seven Sundays, ending with Whitsunday or the Day of Pentecost. The church color for this season is white.

Whitsuntide — begins fifty days after Easter and emphasizes the advent of the Holy Spirit. The Sunday after Whitsunday is known as Trinity Sunday. This entire period, ranging from eleven to sixteen weeks, ends with the last Sunday in August. The church color for this season is red.

Kingdomtide — begins with the first Sunday in September and extends to the time of Advent. Its emphasis is that of the total work of the organized church of God on this earth. There is no particular church color for this season, although green is most generally used.

C. *Conducting Techniques.* Another most important musical area in which a music director must seek to develop himself is in his techniques of conducting. This means first of all a mastery of the conventional conducting patterns, which are shown in outline for the right hand as follows:

2 beat pattern for such time signatures as 2/2 or "Cut Time"; 2/4; or a fast 6/8 which goes in two.

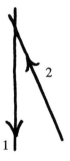

3 beat pattern for such time signatures as 3/2; 3/4; 3/8; and 9/4 or 9/8 when it goes in three.

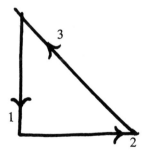

4 beat pattern for such time signatures as 4/2; 4/4; 4/8; and 12/4 or 12/8 when it goes in four.

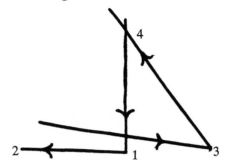

6 beat pattern for such time signatures as 6/2; 6/4; or 6/8 when the tempo is slow and the emphasis is given individual words.

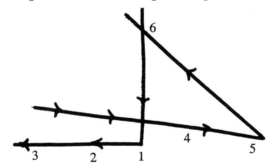

Although the right hand is the main hand for conducting the pattern and keeping rhythm, a director must also learn to do this with his left hand as well. The directions for the left hand conducting patterns are shown as follows:

2 beat pattern for left hand

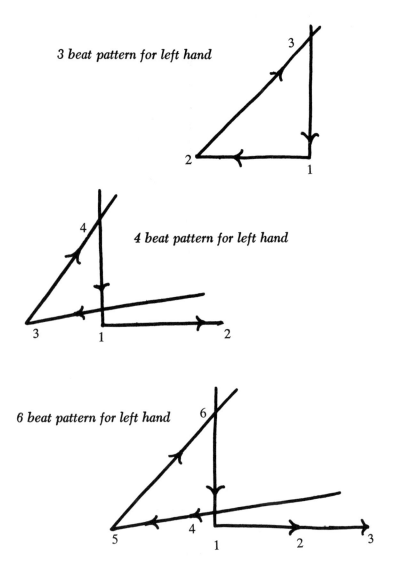

3 beat pattern for left hand

4 beat pattern for left hand

6 beat pattern for left hand

Actually, these diagrams represent only the barest outlines of the conducting patterns. In addition to having the proper directions for the beats, there must also be a feeling of rebound, a sense of expressiveness between the beats, and a preparation given for the next beat. For example, a complete two beat pattern for the right hand would appear as follows:

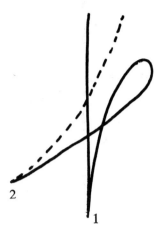

Example — songs using this pattern: "Joy to the World," "Jesus Loves Me."

The complete three beat pattern for the right hand is as follows:

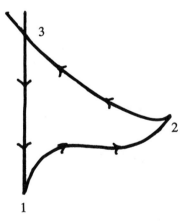

Example — songs using this pattern: "Faith of Our Fathers," "America."

The complete four beat pattern for the right hand is as follows:

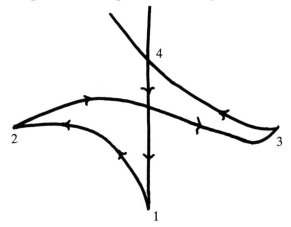

Example — songs using this pattern: "My Faith Looks Up to Thee," "What a Friend We Have in Jesus."

The complete six beat pattern for the right hand is as follows:

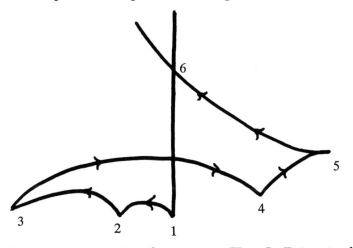

Example — songs using this pattern: "Day Is Dying in the West," "Near the Cross."

The poise and posture of the director are especially important. The suggestion is generally given for beginning directors to clench the fists and to allow the arms to hang naturally at one's side. The arms should then be brought straight up and bent at the elbows and the fists easily opened and relaxed so that the palms are facing the floor and the fingers curved in a graceful manner. It has well been said that a conductor's hands reveal his personality, his sensitiveness to the song, and his command of the situation. Each director must also find that position on the forward part of his feet that makes for maximum ease and gracefulness of his bodily movements.

Before beginning any song, a director must first of all have the hand positions and facial expressions that are necessary to bring his group to keen attention. This anticipatory position must then be followed by a preparatory or breathing motion given in the same tempo of the song to follow. If either the anticipation movement or the preparatory beat is poor, a director can invariably expect a poor attack from his group. Once the group is started and singing, the director's pattern must be maintained with such subconsciousness that he can devote his main attention to his singers, helping them with such matters as catching the proper mood of the song, entrances, releases, shadings, and the other interpretative demands of the music.

The mood and interpretative demands of a song also determine the size or extent of the arm movements that a conductor uses in directing a song. For example, a song requiring bigness and grandeur would be conducted with the largest unit a director has at his disposal, the arm to the fingers acting as one total unit. A song that is moderate in tempo and smooth in character would be directed primarily from the elbow to the fingers. A song that is fast and light or has a staccato movement would be directed primarily from just the wrist to the fingers. It should be emphasized, moreover, that a director's entire being — facial expressions, muscular tensions, as well as the arm and hand movements — all must combine as a total force in making the desired effects obvious to each singer. It should be noted that in all of one's directing there must be a sense of gracefulness, naturalness and control over bodily movements. The task of each director in developing his conducting technique, therefore, is to eliminate every mannerism that detracts from his effectiveness and to learn to make even the slightest movement as meaningful as possible. The mark of a good conductor is that he can achieve maximum results with minimum effort.

The releases or cut-offs in a song are indicated with the following movements:

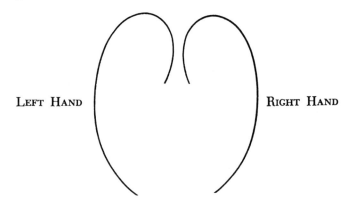

LEFT HAND   RIGHT HAND

Another phase of conducting technique that needs special development is the indication of clear attacks and voice part cues. As mentioned previously, good attacks are dependent upon: (1) establishing the proper mental attitude for singing, (2) getting the group's keen attention before ever attempting any singing, (3) giving a good preparatory beat or motion in the exact tempo of the song that makes the group imitate the director's own breathing preparation, and (4) a clear, definite beat for the attack. When the song begins on the first or down-beat of a measure, the preparatory beat should be an upward motion similar to the upbeat motion in a conducting pattern. When the song begins on the upbeat, the preparatory beat should be an outward motion similar to the position given the third beat in a four beat pattern. If a song should begin on a beat other than the first or last beats of a measure, the preparatory beat should be similar to that used if the song were starting on the down-beat, with the attack beginning right on the beat of the pattern for which the song begins. For example, the song "Finlandia" or the hymn "Be Still, My Soul," adapted from it, begins on the second beat of a four beat measure. The preparatory beat for this song will be the same as though it were starting on a down-beat, with the conductor's attack beginning right on the second beat and the regular four beat pattern then continued throughout the song.

When a song begins on the last half or the "and" of any beat, the preparatory motion should be given where the main stress of that beat is normally placed, with the "and" attack indicated with a strong, outward wrist movement. For example, the song "In My Heart There Rings a Melody" starts on the last half of the third beat in a four beat measure song. In this case the preparatory beat would be given on the third beat with the actual attack for the "and" indicated with a strong flick of the wrist movement. The regular four beat pattern would then continue throughout the song.

Cues for various part entrances within a song are also indicated with a flexible wrist action. Proper wrist action, then, is important to any director both in his directing as well as in cueing. It should be cautioned, however, that wrists should never become "floppy" in one's conducting. Although the wrists should never be stiff, yet they must have relaxed tension in order to indicate command. When a voice part entrance is on the main part of any beat, the indication should be given with a downward flick of the wrist. When the entrance is on the "and" of any beat, the indication should be that of an upward flick of the wrist. Again it should be stressed that voice part cues must have a preparatory motion given in the tempo of the song whereby the singers are able to anticipate the actual flick of the wrist. In addition to the cueing motion, a director must also look at the part he is cueing. Normally voice part cueing is done with the left hand. However, when this becomes difficult or awkward, it is often necessary to cue with the right hand as well.

Conducting techniques are basically the same for either congregational singing or choir directing. However, in congregational singing the emphasis is on getting quantity of tone and spontaneous interpretation. In choir directing, the emphasis is on quality of tone and interpretation that includes precision and more subtlety. Consequently, in congregational singing the movements are much bigger and broader, with both hands often duplicating each other for the sake of emphasis. Here the director's main concern is in setting appropriate tempos and in keeping the congregation rhythmically together on each word. In choir directing, each hand has individual importance. The right hand is primarily the rhythm or pattern hand while the left hand is used especially for interpretation and cueing. For indicating crescendos, the open palm of the left hand would normally be used while the down palm would be used for indicating decrescendos. However, it should be stressed that a director must learn to direct, cue and get desired musical effects with either hand.

D. *Other Conducting Patterns.* Occasionally a director encounters music with time signatures that require different conducting patterns. These patterns are shown for the right hand as follows:

A 9/4 or 9/8 song that moves slowly, giving an emphasis to the words and to each beat within the measure.

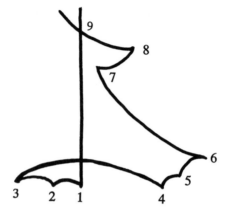

A 12/4 or 12/8 song that moves slowly, giving an emphasis to the words and to each beat within the measure.

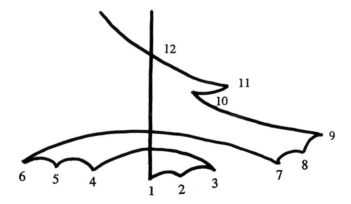

An 8/2, 8/4, or 8/8 meter song.

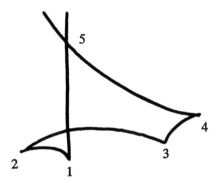

A five beat song in which the word and rhythm accents divide the notes into groups of two plus three.

A five beat song in which the word and rhythm accents divide the notes into groups of three plus two.

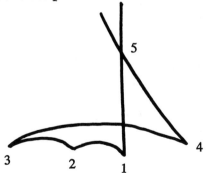

A seven beat song in which the word and rhythm accents divide the notes into groups of three plus four.

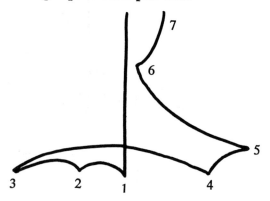

A seven beat song in which the word and rhythm accents divide the notes into groups of four plus three.

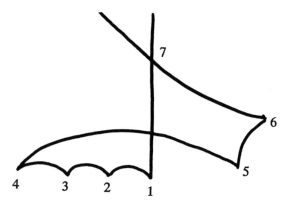

E. *Divided and Collected Beats.* There is still another phase of conducting technique to which a director must give attention. This is the use of divided and collected beats. The use of either is dependent upon the tempo of a song. For a song that moves slowly, it is impossible to control a group using the regular conducting patterns. For example, a song that has four beats to a measure but moves in a slow tempo would have to be subdivided in order to maintain rhythmic control. This could be done by using either the eight beat pattern or a divided four beat pattern with emphasized wrist action as follows:

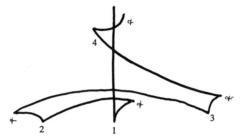

Generally, most directors use the emphasized wrist action to divide a beat. However, the choice of either method for dividing a beat will depend to a large extent upon the amount of stress and the type of pulsations within the song.

Collected beats are used for rhythms that move too rapidly to use the regular beat patterns. For example, a three beat song that moves too rapidly to direct in the regular three beat pattern should be conducted with just one beat to a measure. A four beat song that moves too rapidly to make the regular four beat pattern possible should be directed with a two beat pattern ("cut-time"). A six beat song that moves rapidly would be conducted with a two beat pattern, thus giving three secondary pulsations to each main beat. Example — "Showers of Blessing." A nine beat song that moves rapidly would be conducted with a three beat pattern. Example — "Blessed Assurance." A twelve beat song that moves rapidly would be conducted with a four beat pattern. Examples — "Saved, Saved"; "More Holiness Give Me." For the purpose of getting a greater emphasis on particular words or to achieve a more definite climax, a director may change from the collected beat idea to that of directing and emphasizing each individual beat.

The use of divided, regular or collected beat patterns can be illustrated as follows:

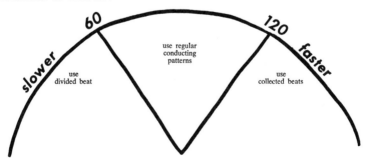

When a tempo is between 60 to 120 pulsations per minute, the regular conducting patterns can be used. When the tempo is less than 60 pulsations per minute, a director should use the divided beat patterns. When the tempo is more than 120 pulsations per minute, the collected beat idea should be used. A director can determine a 60 tempo from either a metronome, the second hand on his watch, or by saying the word "MISSISSIPPI" at a moderate rate. Naturally, a 120 tempo would be just twice this fast, etc.

F. *An Understanding of Voices.* It has well been said that the human voice is the choicest of all musical instruments, with all other instruments mere imitations of the voice. Since church music is primarily vocal, it is important that a church music director learn all that he can about voice culture.

First of all, a director should know the vocal ranges that are average for each voice part. These are shown as follows:

SOPRANOS   ALTOS   TENORS   BASSES

The range of a voice is generally defined as the highest pure and lowest pure tones that are singable by a particular voice. However, a director must understand not only the range factor in working with voices, but he must also be conscious of the quality, color or timbre of each voice as well. Voices are further classified according to vocal quality as follows:

Sopranos
1. Coloratura — a bright, light quality, capable of singing in very high ranges.
2. Lyric — a pure, smooth quality.
3. Dramatic — a full, heavier quality.
4. Mezzo — fullness which approaches a contralto's quality, especially in the mezzo's middle range.

Altos
1. Lyric or high altos — a pure, smooth quality.
2. Contraltos — a full, heavy, resonant quality, especially in the lower register.

Tenors
1. Lyric — a pure, high, light quality.
2. Dramatic — a fuller, heavier quality.

Basses
1. Baritones — a voice with a wide, colorful range.
2. Bass-baritone — rich, firm low tones not characteristic of a baritone.
3. Bass or Bass Profundo — a heavy, resonant quality, capable of singing tones in the contra-bass range.

A church music director should learn, then, how to work with and develop all types of voices. This would include giving singers tone and vowel consciousness, diction techniques, a uniform, resonant quality throughout their entire range, a keen awareness of pitch and intonation, as well as the underlying principles of effective interpretation. A music director must first, however, experience these concepts himself under the guidance of a capable voice teacher before he can expect to impart these same ideals to others.

It must be the constant desire of a church music director to improve his talents and techniques. Reading periodicals and books on various aspects of music, attending workshops and music clinics, as well as sharing ideas with other directors are all helpful aids in one's musical development. Membership in one or more professional organizations is also an invaluable help in this regard. Several of these organizations include:

American Guild of English Handbell Ringers
100 W. Tenth St., Wilmington, Delaware 19899

American Guild of Organists
630 Fifth Ave., New York, N.Y. 10020

Christian Artists
P.O. Box 1984, Thousand Oaks, California 91360

The Choristers' Guild
440 N. Lake Center, Dallas, Texas 75238

The Hymn Society of America
c/o Texas Christian University
Ed Landreth Hall
2900 So. University Dr., Fort Worth, Texas 76129

G. *List of Music Publishers.* One of the difficult jobs of any church music director is finding a continuous supply of new and suitable music. A working relationship with the various music publishing houses can be of real help in this regard. It is suggested when ordering music from any publisher that a director list the name of the song, composer or arranger or editor, the publisher's order number, the voice parts (SATB, SAB, SSA, TTBB, SA, etc.) and the number of copies desired. Upon request, publishers will send a catalogue to a music director and will usually send a sample copy of the music on approval as well. The following list of music publishers is given for reference:

Alexandria House
P.O. Box 300
Alexandria, IN 46001

Associated Music Publ., Inc.
866 Third Ave.
New York, NY 10022

Augsburg Publ. House
426 South 5th Street
Minneapolis, MN 55415

Belwin-Mills Publ. Corp.
25 Deshon Drive
Melvile, NY 11746

Benson, John T. Publ. Co.
1625 Broadway
Nashville, TN 37202

Big Three Music Corp.
Meadow Lands Ave.
Lyndhurst, NJ 07071

Boosey Hawkes
P.O. Box 130
Oceanside, NY 11572

Boston Music Co.
116 Boylston St.
Boston, MA 02116

Bourne, Inc.
866 Third Ave.
New York, NY 10022

Broadman Press
127 N. 9th Ave.
Nashville, TN 37203

Choral Press
251 W. 19th St.
New York, NY 10011

Concordia Publ. House
3558 S. Jefferson Ave.
St. Louis, MO 63118

Crescendo Music Publ., Inc.
2580 Gus Thomasson Rd.
P.O. Box 28218
Dallas, TX 75228

Elkan-Vogel Co., Inc.
Presser Place
Bryn Mawr, PA 19010

Fischer, Carl, Inc.
56-62 Cooper Square
New York, NY 10003

Fischer and Bro., J.
(order from Belwin-Mills Co.)

Sam Fox Publ. Co.
170 N.E. 33rd St.
Ft. Lauderdale, FL 33334

Gaither Music Co.
(order from Alexandria House)

Galaxy Music Corp.
112 South St.
Boston, MA 02111

Good Life Productions
7901 E. Pierce St.
Scottsdale, AZ 85257

Gospel Publ. House
1445 Booneville Ave.
Springfield, MO 65802

Gray Co., Inc. H. W.
(order from Belwin-Mills Co.)

Hinshaw Music Press
Box 802
Dayton, OH 45401

Hope Publishing Co.
Carol Stream, IL 60187

Kendor Music, Inc.
Box 278
Delevan, NY 14042

Kjos Music Co., Neil
4382 Jutland Dr.
San Diego, CA 92117

Lexicon Music Co.
P.O. Box 2222
Newbury Park, CA 91320

Lillenas Publ. Co.
Box 527
Kansas City, KS 64141

Lorenz Publ. Co.
501 E. Third St.
Dayton, OH 45401

Ludwig Music Co.
557-59 E. 140th St.
Cleveland, OH 44110

Manna Music Co.
2111 Kenmere Ave.
Burbank, CA 91504

Morris, Edwin H. and Co.
729 Seventh Ave.
New York, NY 10019

Musical Ministries
P.O. Box 5378
Greenville, SC 29606

Peters, C. F. Corp
373 Park Ave. South
New York, NY 10016

Presser, Theodore, Co.
Presser Place
Bryn Mawr, PA 19010

Pro Art Music Publishers
469 Union Ave.
Westbury, Long Island, NY 11591

G. Ricordi and Co.
866 Third Ave.
New York, NY 10022

RobinSong Publ. Co.
4309 Idylwild Terrace
Marshall, TX 75670

E. C. Schirmer Music Co.
112 South St.
Boston, MA 02111

G. Schirmer Co.
866 Third Ave.
Westbury, Long Island, NY 10022

Shawnee Press, Inc.
Delaware Water Gap, PA 18327

Singspiration, Inc.
315 Richard Terrace S.E.
Grand Rapids, MI 49506

Southern Music Publ. Co.
1100 Broadway, Box 329
San Antonio, TX 78206

Sparrow/Birdwing Music Co.
8025 Deering Ave.
Canoga Park, CA 91304

Summy-Birchard Co.
Box CN 27
Princeton, NJ 08540

Tempo Music Publ.
2712 W. 104th Terr.
Leawood, KS 66206

Triune Music Co.
P.O. Box 23088
824 19th Ave. S.
Nashville, TN 37202

Volkwein Brothers, Inc.
117 Sandusky St.
Pittsburgh, PA 15212

Willis Music Co.
7380 Industrial Rd.
Florence, KY 41042

Word, Inc.
Box 1790
Waco, TX 76703

ASSIGNMENTS

1. Discuss what you consider to be the most important qualifications for a church music director.
2. Express in your own words the basic differences between a hymn and a gospel song.
3. Choose ten appropriate songs for each of the following services in the church:
   a. Sunday evening gospel service
   b. Sunday morning worship service
   c. Midweek prayer service
   d. Sunday school exercises
   e. Young people's meeting
4. Discuss all that is involved in developing a good conducting technique. Point out the differences between congregational song leading and choral directing.
5. State the conducting pattern that you would use for each of the following songs:
   a. "Nothing But the Blood"
   b. "The Solid Rock"
   c. "The Old Rugged Cross"
   d. "There Shall Be Showers of Blessing"
   e. "Blessed Assurance"
   f. "Make Me a Blessing"
   g. "Have Thine Own Way, Lord"
   h. "Saved, Saved!"
   i. "More Like the Master"
   j. "I Need Jesus"

ADDITIONAL READING

1. *A Choir Director's Handbook.* Compiled by Andrea Wells Miller. Published by Word, Inc.
2. *Choral Conducting* by Davison. Published by Harvard University Press.
3. *Chorus Conducting from Organization to Performance* by Krone. Published by Kjos Co.
4. *Church Music for the Glory of God* by Urang. Published by the Christian Service Foundation, Moline, Illinois.
5. *Essentials in Conducting* by Gehrkens. Published by Presser Co.
6. *How to Build an Evangelistic Church Music Program* by Terry. Published by Thomas Nelson.
7. *The Ministry of Music in the Church* by Vic Delamont. Published by Moody Press.

3 | CONGREGATIONAL SINGING

A church music director has a twofold responsibility: That of giving every member in the congregation a touch of musical experience, and that of further developing the especially talented. Neither responsibility should be neglected. It is with congregational singing that a music director can exert his musical influence over the greatest number of people at any one time. This is the starting point in developing a vital, total music program in a church. Once the entire congregation is reached with musical inspiration, the task of recruiting and developing other groups becomes much easier.

Psychologists tell us that singing is a natural human behavior and is basically enjoyed by everyone. Congregational singing, then, is not only beneficial to the individual, but active congregational participation in a service should always be one of the chief distinguishing characteristics of evangelical Protestantism. Congregational singing is one of the most important expressions of one of the basic tenets of the evangelical position, that of the priesthood of the individual believer. This principle was one of the important issues in the Reformation movement of the fifteenth and sixteenth centuries. In our church life today there is no finer sight than a congregation of believers heartily enjoying this great heritage.

I. Objectives of a Song Service
(Ephesians 5:19; Colossians 3:16)

A song service for any service should have several basic objectives. A song leader must continually be aware of these objectives and keenly desirous of accomplishing these spiritual ideals. Without this awareness and desire a song service can easily become either sheer entertainment or a mere time-consuming activity. The following are several of these spiritual objectives of a song service:

1. A song service should provide the means of unifying a group by providing a common channel for individuals to join together in worship, prayer and praise.

2. A song service should teach and reinforce spiritual truths.

3. A song service should provide individuals with an outlet for expressions of personal soul attitudes and experiences which often are difficult to express in one's own words.

4. A song service should create the proper mood for the message and the remainder of the service.

II. SOME GENERAL OBSERVATIONS ABOUT CONGREGATIONAL SINGING

It is often said that the spiritual status of a church can be gauged by its congregational singing. It is further contended that great periods in church history, periods of revival and spiritual fervor, have always been characterized by great hymn singing. It must be admitted, however, that today in many of our evangelical churches congregational singing is not in a healthy state. For the most part, congregational singing is either a giddy, superficial, emotional activity or has degenerated into an experience to be endured.

How different would be the singing in our churches today if worshipers would heed the directions for congregational singing given by John Wesley over 200 years ago:[1]

SING ALL. See that you join with the congregation as frequently as you can. Let not a slight degree of weakness or weariness hinder you. If it is a cross to you, take it up, and you will find it a blessing.

SING LUSTILY, and with a good courage. Beware of singing as if you are half-dead or half-asleep; but lift up your voice with strength. Be no more afraid of your voice now, nor more ashamed of it being heard, than when you sing the songs of Satan.

SING MODESTLY. Do not bawl, so as to be heard above or distinct from the rest of the congregation — that you may not destroy the harmony — but strive to unite your voices together so as to make one clear melodious sound.

SING IN TIME. Whatever time is sung, be sure to keep with it. Do not run before nor stay behind it; but attend close to the leading voices, and move therewith as exactly as you can; and take care not to sing too slowly. This drawling way naturally steals on all who are lazy; and it is high time to drive it out from among us, and sing our tunes as quick as we did at first.

ABOVE ALL, SING SPIRITUALLY. Have an eye to God in every word you sing. Aim at pleasing Him more than yourself or any other creature. In order to do this attend strictly to the sense of what you sing, and see that your heart is not carried away with

---

[1]*The Works of John Wesley,* Vol. XIV (Grand Rapids: Zondervan Publishing House), p. 346.

the sound, but offered to God continually; so shall your singing be such as the Lord will approve of here, and reward you when He cometh in the clouds of heaven.

This lack of enthusiastic, meaningful congregational singing cannot be blamed entirely on the parishioner in the pew, however. For the most part the blame must be assumed by the church's leadership in that it has failed to maintain the inspiration and respect for this important area of church activity. There are church leaders who think of the song service as necessary traditional routine. Others merely tolerate it, regarding it only as a way of using up time until the truly important activity, the sermon. Others use the song service as a means of entertainment, or as a display of a particular group or personality, or as a means of attracting a larger crowd to the service. The true ideal, however, is a realization by each church leader that congregational singing is an integral part of the entire service. Each activity of the service, the congregational singing, special music, Scripture reading, prayers, message, etc., should not attract individual attention, but rather each should combine as a total unit in bringing true spiritual blessing to needy individuals.

This, then, is not a plea for the cheer-leading and showmanship tactics commonly associated with the term "song leader." Rather, it is a desire for the return of sincere, inspired, meaningful leadership of congregational singing by consecrated directors. To accomplish this ideal it would be helpful if every leader of a church service would gain a basic appreciation and understanding of the subject of hymnology. This would include a knowledge of the lives of those who wrote the words of the hymns, something about the times and conditions in which they wrote, the personal experiences that prompted the writing of particular hymns, as well as a knowledge about the origins and composers of the music. For helpful texts, see *Singing with Understanding* by Kenneth W. Osbeck, published by Kregel Publications; *The Story of Christian Hymnology* by E. E. Ryden, published by Augustana Press; *Hymn Tune Names* by Robert Guy McCutcham, published by Abingdon Press. It is also good for a leader to encourage his people to use their hymnals along with their Bibles and other devotional materials in their personal devotions. This deeper perception of hymn appreciation will do much to relieve the flippant style of congregational singing or the stolid, sluggish type of singing found in many congregations. When people are sincerely alerted to the possibilities of spiritual enrichments from hymnody, they will respond and "sing with the spirit, and . . . with the understanding also" (I Corinthians 14:15).

In a more formal worship service a music director's influence over congregational singing is not as strong as it is in a more informal, evangelistic type of service. Even in the worship service, however, there are items that a director can discuss with the pastor and accompanist that will make for more meaningful singing. The director can remind the pastor of hymns that are especially appropriate for worship and easy to sing, hymns that are especially difficult to sing, hymns that are too commonly used, or unfamiliar hymns that the congregation should learn. In this regard it can be helpful if the music director knows of such hymns in advance and has the choir ready to lead the congregation forcefully in the learning of such songs.

An especially important person and one who is vitally responsible for good congregational singing is the organist. A music director must realize the importance of this person and work in close co-operation with him. By having occasional informal discussions on such topics as the purposes of church music, items of interest regarding a hymn or an anthem, improvements in the order of service, etc., an amateur organist's entire philosophy of church music may be heightened and his sensitivity to the needs and moods of a service improved. Often an organist with years of experience will discover for the first time the thrill of creatively playing the emotional meanings of the words of each verse of a hymn rather than being content merely with the exactness of the music.

III. Specific Suggestions for the Song Leader

It is in the area of more informal congregational singing such as the traditional evening service that a director can exert the greatest influence in getting people to sing. This type of leadership requires much skill and wisdom if it is to be done effectively. To the song leader falls the responsibility of realizing the spiritual objectives of the song service. He must become a keen student of crowd psychology. As the leader he must unify and inspire the audience as well as guide the necessary mechanics of a service. Yet all of this must be done so that the message of the music and the spiritual emphasis of the service are the focal points of attraction rather than the leader himself.

The following are specific suggestions offered to song leaders to encourage better congregational singing:

1. Be thoroughly prepared for the service. Be well on time for the service. Know in advance such matters as the verses of a song to be used or omitted, when the audience will

stand, etc. Pray earnestly for God's guidance and blessing on the singing portion of the service.

2. Direct the service in an enthusiastic and friendly manner, yet with mature dignity. The proper position for the song leader is generally to the right of the pulpit, although this position must never become fixed or stereotyped.

3. Establish a personal, sympathetic contact with your audience. Know the words and music of a song well enough so that you aren't tied to the book.

4. Use the conventional conducting patterns and techniques discussed in the previous chapter. Have a definite downbeat for each measure. Make all conducting movements positive, yet graceful. Avoid peculiarities and mannerisms in your conducting, such as stiffness, pointing of the index finger, etc. (An excellent means for eliminating these mannerisms is the frequent use of a mirror.)

5. Make the size and extent of the arm movements comparable to the size of the audience, the mood of the song, and the type of service being conducted.

6. Be tempo and rhythm conscious. Regardless of a song's mood, it must be directed with enough "lift" to make it singable.

7. Always carry the melody of the song when leading with the voice. When this becomes vocally impossible, sing a harmony part under the congregation, never the melody an octave lower.

8. Lead with your voice as well as with the conducting pattern when beginning each new verse or to pick up a lagging phrase. Conserve yourself, however, when the congregation is enthusiastically singing (yet continue to show interest), so that when it is necessary to speak you have not made yourself hoarse or breathless.

9. Be the song leader and not the preacher. Don't feel that you have to say a great deal between every verse or between the songs, yet be able to give a meaningful word about the song when it is appropriate.

10. Strive to have a lively and interesting voice quality for giving instructions. Speak slowly and firmly enough to be distinct. When announcing a hymn give the instructions at least twice. (Remember, your speaking voice is a vital factor in expressing your personality.)

11. Guard against annoying mannerisms and expressions in your speaking. This includes flagrant grammatical errors or ambiguous expressions such as, "Let us stand as we sing,"

or, "hymn number two hundred *and* sixty." (This could mean singing two different songs.) Also avoid mispronunciations such as peé-un-ist rather than pee-an-ist for "pianist," etc.

12. Don't wear out the audience by excessive standing and singing. (Generally plan to have the audience stand twice before the message.) Give opportunities to rest occasionally or to enjoy some other activity. Give enough time between verses of a song for the congregation to catch a breath so as to begin together on the new verse.

13. Don't get into a rut with your congregation. Don't use the the same songs all of the time. (It is a good plan to keep a record of the songs you use.) Avoid using the same approach or the same expressions for beginning each service or for introducing each song.

14. Know your own church hymnal thoroughly. Strive to memorize as many songs as you can. (This always makes for the most effective directing.) It is also helpful to prepare a list of songs that are suitable for all types of services and which are found in most hymnals.

15. Try new techniques and ideas that you have seen others use successfully. However, never imitate a certain person. Be natural — be yourself.

16. Use special effects or "stunts" with extreme care and caution. Never allow these practices to let a service get out of control or to cause embarrassment to anyone. Some of these song leading practices include: dramatic pauses, sudden changes in tempo, undue holding of certain notes, antiphonal singing (one section of the audience answering another group), pitting one group of singers against another, using choruses with rounds, the use of whistling or clapping of hands, etc.

17. Work with the pastor so that the entire service emphasizes a common theme and all of the songs and activities have the same basic purpose.

18. Never allow the service to become dull and monotonous. Be inspirational. Use contrast and variety between numbers as well as between the verses of a song. Be ready for and make something of the climaxes when they occur within a song.

19. Women directors — be enthusiastic but remain feminine at all times.

20. Keep a sense of movement to the service, yet make the audience feel relaxed.

IV. ATTRACTING INTEREST FOR THE SONG SERVICE

Always a challenge for any song leader is the matter of starting the service. It is the director's responsibility to say or do the right thing so that the audience becomes quickly unified and ready to sing. There is an interesting Greek proverb which says, "The beginning is the half of all things," or "Well begun, half done." There is usually a great deal of initial inertia that must be overcome with any audience. Basic, of course, is the fact that a song leader must project a spirit of sincere enthusiasm that soon becomes contagious with the entire group. Most song leaders, however, use various planned approaches for beginning each song service. Some of these approaches are listed briefly as follows:

1. A warm, friendly greeting and welcome to the audience.
2. A short, personal, enthusiastic testimony which leads directly into the first song.
3. Quoting a Scripture passage which has to do with singing. For example: Psalm 149:1; Colossians 3:16; Ephesians 5:19.
4. Quoting a verse of the first hymn to be used, then having the congregation join in spontaneously without their hymnals.
5. Beginning with prayer, asking God's blessing upon this particular service.
6. Having a theme song or chorus for a special period of time.
7. Beginning with an unannounced special number, either instrumental or vocal.
8. Beginning with a "musical package" — several special numbers together without any announcement between each.
9. Immediately asking the congregation to stand for the first song and to remain standing for prayer.
10. Having the choir sing a verse and chorus of a familiar song, such as "Wonderful Grace of Jesus," followed by the chorus repeated in a soft hum, during which time the pastor or song leader leads in opening prayer.

V. MAINTAINING INTEREST THROUGHOUT THE SONG SERVICE

As is true in any program building, a song leader must develop a keen sense of the factors involved in maintaining an audience's interest and attention. Once interest lags or an audience becomes restless, it usually is a difficult task to recapture that attention during the remainder of the service. A song leader must not only capture an audience's attention and maintain that interest throughout the song service, but he must actually build that interest so that the people are prepared and eager to receive the spoken word.

An audience's interest is maintained as a song leader is able to achieve a balance of unity and variety within a song service. Although there should be a unified theme throughout the service, a director should be aware of choosing songs with contrasting tempos, moods and rhythms. Songs should be selected so that a change of key is possible when moving from one song to the next. Special music such as soloists and various musical groups within the church can also be used to give relief from continuous singing as well as to provide greater variety and interest. The following additional suggestions are offered as possible helps for maintaining interest within a song service:

1. Use various groups of people or sections of the congregation to sing or play various verses or parts of a song.
2. Use medleys — a chain of several songs or songs and choruses, for the purpose of getting the people to respond spontaneously.
3. Occasionally give the story or background about the song or perhaps some interesting incident associated with the use of the song in the past.
4. Occasionally have just the voices sing unaccompanied.
5. Occasionally have the audience merely read the words of a verse of a song or perhaps hum while the words are read or as a soloist sings the words, etc.
6. Occasionally have the accompanist raise the key by a half step for a verse of a song in order to achieve greater exhilaration for those words when appropriate.
7. Occasionally have "Audience Favorites" — just one verse of various individuals' favorite hymns.
8. Have the congregation learn and try to appreciate new or unfamiliar hymns by having a hymn of the month. (It is always good to have a definite and practical plan for learning new songs and choruses each month.)
9. Occasionally have a service with a song sermon. An entire service of congregational singing based on a common theme, "heaven," "peace," "assurance," etc., or perhaps a program of songs all written by the same hymn writer.
10. Use an appropriate poem, humorous story or anecdote when in good taste.

VI. TEACHING NEW CHORUSES

With regard to choosing and teaching new gospel choruses to an audience as part of a song service, the following suggestions are given:

1. The words of the chorus should be simple, should contain a sound Scriptural truth or have a significant Scriptural thought.
2. The melody and rhythm of the chorus should lend themselves to easy learning.
3. Know the chorus perfectly before trying to teach others. It is always wise to have a copy of the words regardless of how well one may think he knows the chorus.
4. Be sure the accompanist has a copy of the music and has had an opportunity to play the chorus before the time of the service.
5. It will be helpful for a director to make his own collection of choruses based on various subjects — praise, prayer, consecration, etc.
6. A procedure for teaching a short chorus:
   a. Give an introduction to the chorus so that a desire is created for the audience to learn the chorus.
   b. Give the words while the accompanist plays the music.
   c. Sing the chorus for the congregation, or possibly have the choir or others ready to help you sing.
   d. Repeat the words again without music.
   e. Have the congregation try it through while you help by singing above them, inserting a word or phrase just before they sing it, and by indicating with your hand the direction of the melody.
   f. Have the congregation repeat the chorus several times but have a valid reason for requesting each repetition.
   g. Review this chorus the next week.
7. A procedure for teaching a longer chorus:
   a. Give an introduction for the chorus.
   b. Give all of the words while the accompanist plays the music.
   c. Sing the entire chorus for the congregation.
   d. Repeat all of the words again without music.
   e. Sing just the first phrase or section of the chorus again with the congregation repeating this phrase after you.
   f. Repeat this procedure of learning each phrase or section of the chorus separately until the entire chorus is completed.
   g. Sing the entire chorus.
   h. Review the next week.

8. Don't spend too much time on a chorus during the first learning. It is always better to review the chorus the following Sunday than to kill the interest during the first learning.

VII. CONCLUSION

What greater privilege could a church music director desire than the opportunity of providing a common channel for all individuals of the congregation to join together in expressions of worship, prayer and praise, and in so doing to find spiritual enrichment for their lives. It should be remembered, moreover, that the message of a song often reaches certain individuals with the Gospel or some spiritual encouragement that might never be gained by other parts of the church service. Such possibilities are responsibilities that a music director must never take lightly.

ASSIGNMENTS

1. Discuss in your own words the spiritual objectives of a song service.
2. Discuss what the true role of the song leader should be in a service.
3. Discuss the various suggestions given to aid song leaders in encouraging better congregational singing. What are some of the most glaring weaknesses you have noted with most amateur song leaders?
4. Discuss various techniques for capturing, maintaining and building audience attention and interest throughout a song service.
5. Prepare a complete order of service for a Sunday evening gospel meeting, showing your approach to the service, the songs to be used and the various activities to be included.

ADDITIONAL READING

1. *Community and Assembly Singing* by Zanzig. Published by M. Witmark & Sons.
2. *Forty Approaches to Informal Singing* by Frieswyk. Published by the National Recreation Association, New York.
3. *Lead a Song! A Practical Guide to the Organization and Conducting of Informal Group Singing* by Wilson. Published by Hall & McCreary Co.
4. *Song Leadership* by Rodeheaver and Ford. Published by The Rodeheaver Co.

4 | CHILDREN'S CHOIRS

Any church music director with vision realizes that not only must he develop the "faithful few" in the senior choir, but he must train a group of consecrated musicians for future use in the service of the church. If the church music program is to be perpetuated, he must begin at once to lay the necessary ground work for a total music program. It is true that not all of his ideals will be realized immediately, but a director must begin with over-all objectives before he can successfully attain specific goals. Obviously, the starting point in building a total church music program for the future is with the children of the church. Working with children offers more possibility of rewarding satisfactions for a director than perhaps any other age group, since the average child will thoroughly enjoy and respond to music if it is properly presented. There are, however, certain prerequisites that are basic for a director of a children's choir:

1. A genuine love for children.
2. The ability to make children respond willingly.
3. The ability to administer the choirs creatively and imaginatively.
4. The qualities of patience, tact and understanding.
5. A basic knowledge of music, children's voices and conducting techniques.
6. A desire to enrich children's lives through the participation in and the enjoyment of music.
7. A desire to improve the music situation in our churches through a long-range program of Christian education.
8. A vision of the opportunities for winning children to Christ and of molding in them a Christian character.

The discussion in this chapter will consider the organization, administration and musical instruction of children's choirs for the ages of four through twelve.

I. BEGINNERS' CHOIR

The Beginners' Choir is for boys and girls four and five years of age or those of pre-school and kindergarten age. This choir does not ordinarily perform in public, except, perhaps, for special occasions such as Sunday school Christmas programs, etc. The basic purpose for such a group is educational — to give the child some fundamental concepts regarding music, especially its use in the worship and service of God.

In order to establish a choir program for a child of this age, it is well to know in advance something of his behavior patterns and characteristics. The beginner's family and their events will constitute his main world. He is just beginning to discover the outside world. Often he will view with caution and suspicion such new ventures as a choir rehearsal until he becomes accustomed to it. His physical co-ordination is still limited since the small muscles for fine co-ordination have not yet been developed. Consequently, one must use activities involving large movements. The attention span of this child is limited. His learning is done principally by imitation. He best understands and learns new material when comparisons are made with truths that are already familiar to him. His sense of imagination is great. Children of this age do not like a competitive approach. If there are to be prizes, there must be prizes for all.

Beginner choir music should be characterized by brevity and repetition. Some of the most effective songs and choruses are not more than eight measures long. The ideal leader's voice would be the lyric soprano, although any voice properly used can be utilized. All songs are taught by imitation and rote. The approach for teaching a new song is an informal one, with the director striving for as much spontaneity from the children as possible. A suggested procedure for teaching rote songs to beginners is as follows:

1. Give the motivation for the song. Begin a conversation about the song or some points of interest regarding it that will in turn create a desire for the children to learn the song.
2. Sing the entire song for the children.
3. Explain any of the words that might be difficult to understand.
4. Speak the words in the rhythm of the song.
5. Ask the children to listen for specific points of interest within the song while you sing it for them once again.

6. Talk about the song and the various points of interest the children heard while you were singing.

7. Sing the first phrase or section of the song and have the children repeat it after you.

8. Do the same thing with the second phrase, after which sing both phrases together. Continue this procedure until the entire song is learned. During this singing, help the children find the melody by indicating the direction of the melody with your hand.

9. Sing the song in its entirety. Don't, however, expect or try to achieve perfection during this first learning.

10. Review again at the next rehearsal.

The director of any children's choir should try to achieve a light, clear tone quality throughout the child's entire vocal range. This does not mean that a child must sing with a timid, thin quality. However, at all times a leader should be careful not to cause strain either in getting volume of tone or in singing extreme ranges. The following suggested ranges are considered safe singing ranges for children's voices of various ages:

Pre-school and Kindergarten	First Grade	Second Grade	Third Grade
E-D	E♭-E♭	D-E	C-E

Fourth Grade	Fifth Grade	Sixth Grade
C-F	B-F	B♭ to F and occasional G's

A director must also be conscious of the tessitura problem so that no song remains consistently high or low for any period of time. This too will cause strain and possible harm if not heeded.

The director of the Beginners' Choir is likely to have a number of children who still cannot sing on pitch or carry a tune. This is not unusual, especially if the children have not heard much music in the home. This is the ideal age to correct such problems. Most non-singing children will be corrected simply by being in a singing group. More specific help can be given these children by getting them to distinguish between high and low tones, loud and soft tones, and to imitate sounds that they already know, such as bird sounds, fire engine sirens, and others. The director may also play musical conversations and games with the children, asking them questions on various pitches with the children imitating this pitch with their answers. A helpful book for this type of activity is *Tone Matching Tunes* by Coit and Bampton, published by Flammer Company.

The beginner child should be made rhythm conscious and taught to express pulse and rhythm through bodily responses. His rhythmic expression may be encouraged by marching, running, skipping, swaying and clapping to music when it is played, as well as using various rhythm instruments. When listening to music, beginner children should be able to recognize by ear the note combinations which suggest various physical responses. This would include: walking or marching music — quarter notes; running music — eighth notes; skipping music — dotted eighths and sixteenths; strolling music — half notes; and holding music — whole notes. Beginner youngsters are too young to be taught an arithmetical understanding of note values, so that rhythmic accuracy in their singing is gained only by imitation. The use of activity and motion songs or choruses is helpful for adding interest in a rhythmic activity. It should be cautioned, however, that the spiritual thought of the song must never be misunderstood for the sake of rhythmic activity. It should also be mentioned that songs employing activity and motion must be well learned before any action is attempted. There are various secular books containing rhythmic activities and musical games that a director can use profitably for this purpose: *Twice 55 Games with Music* by Dykema, published by Birchard; *Games for Children*, published by the National Recreational Association, 315 Fourth Ave., New York; *Singing Games for Children* by Hamlin and Guessford, published by Willis Music Company; *Action Songs for Special Occasions* by Newman, published by Mills Music Company; *Rime, Rhythm and Song* by Martin and Burnet, published by Hall and McCreary.

Attitudes of reverence and worship can also begin with Beginners' Choir. Children can be reminded of some of the characteristics of "big church" — soft music, quietness, everyone singing, the meaning of the word "Amen," etc. Proper choral attitudes such as sitting up straight, attentiveness to the director, good attacks and releases may also be taught this age group.

During the 30-35 minute rehearsal, the director must do his best to keep things moving and interesting. A director's prime desire should be to make children enjoy music. It is generally best to have the group seated on small chairs in a circle with the director seated on the same level with them. Rehearsals can include activities such as: singing familiar songs and choruses, learning a new song, rhythmic activities, fun games, listening to records, and perhaps an occasional surprise.

When choosing songs for this age group, a director should

select songs that are geared to the child's limited understanding and vocal abilities. The text of these songs should emphasize God's love and care for His children, truths from the life of Christ, as well as God's revelation in nature. These are truths that children can experience and understand. Songs with a more doctrinal emphasis will generally be beyond the grasp of the child of this age. Songs that tell a story are especially appealing at this time. In general, the texts must have simplicity — but simplicity with charm.

Some of the various collections useful for children of this age are: *When the Little Child Wants to Sing* by Laufer, Westminster Press; *Songs for the Pre-School Age* by Shumate, Broadman Press; *All Through the Year* by Whelan, Hall and McCreary Co.; *Worship and Conduct Songs for Beginners and Primaries* by Shields, John Knox Press, Richmond, Virginia; *Beginners Sing in Church and Home*, Scripture Press; *Add a Song* by Stella B. Daleburn, Lillenas Publishing Co.; *Songs for Pre-School Children* by Paulton, Standard Publishing Co.; *Cherub Choir* by Smith, Singspiration; *God's Wonderful World* (Songs, Hymns and Games) by Mason and Ohaman, Random House, New York.

Suggested names for a Beginners' Choir: Cherub Choir, Angelic Chorus, Celestial Choir, etc.

II. Primary Choir

The Primary Choir is for boys and girls who are six through eight years of age or in the first, second or third grades in school. This choir can be used occasionally in the church services with quite good results. The music, though still taught by rote and sung in unison, is somewhat more involved and interesting than that used for the Beginners' Choir.

Again, before beginning work with this age group, a director should be acquainted with the primary child's behavior patterns and characteristics. This age group is generally active, though still basically self-centered. At this age children become quite conscious of their individual abilities. It is for this reason that a bit of competition and the giving of awards such as ribbons, stars, etc., is a stimulating motivation for various group activities. These children are generally anxious to appear grown up, and this approach has a strong appeal to them. Activities that make use of counting, arithmetic games, etc., are especially appealing. The attention span is noticeably greater with primaries than it is with the beginners. Since primary children have such strong preconceived likes and dislikes, the wise director must learn to present his wishes in such a manner as to make the children enjoy carrying out his desires. This is also the age for "hero worship." It should be the normal experience that these children will simply "love their director." The wise director knows how to use and control this attitude in building a strong rapport between himself and the choir and in so doing establishing a sound choir program.

Not only should the primary choir sing songs with more variety and complexity, but they should be started in the matter of learning something about correct tone production, diction, phrasing, as well as some basic facts about music theory. The child should be able to distinguish between a good tone and a bad one from the standpoint of pitch correctness and quality. A clear head tone quality should be firmly established by the time a child leaves this choir. The vowel sounds "O" and "oo" are good for developing this concept, with the added sensation that this quality is carried *down* rather than, in any way, the lower register quality forced up. These children should also be taught the need for such basic vocal techniques as an open mouth and relaxed jaw, thus providing a free, open throat for their singing. In addition, they should be taught the importance of good posture for supporting their singing. This is vital in teaching them to sing phrase-wise, thus overcoming their natural tendency to take a breath after every few notes. It is also quite common for children to mumble their words as they sing. A helpful technique for improving diction at this age is simply to have the children practice the words of a song in a whisper, impressing upon them the need for using their lips and tongues in saying words clearly. As mentioned previously, the average singing range for this age group is generally from middle C to E. Most authorities are agreed that there is as much danger to correct tone production in having children sing too low as there is in having them sing too high.

Rhythmically, primaries can be expected to achieve much more perfect repetition of rhythmic activities than can be expected from the earlier age group. The entire approach to rhythm is still that of associating physical responses to music rather than attempting any intellectual or arithmetical understanding of rhythm. Through this approach they should begin to realize that the first beat of a measure is always the strongest beat. This can be emphasized by having them march, clap, bounce an imaginary ball, play rhythm instruments to the pulse of different time signatures, etc. Many directors make use of organized rhythm bands in establishing this rhythm consciousness. A helpful book for this is *How to Teach Rhythm Bands* by Diller and Page, published by G. Schirmer.

As mentioned previously, a child's first introduction to a formal study of rhythm should be that of physical response through listening to music. After a sufficient background of listening and responding to music, primary children are ready to begin the recognition of note values with the physical associations and activities they have already experienced with rhythm. A useful technique in this transition stage is the teaching and learning of rhythmic chants. For example, by learning the following chant, the children can associate the activity of "walking" with quarter notes, "strolling" with half notes, and then can be shown what these notes look like when printed.

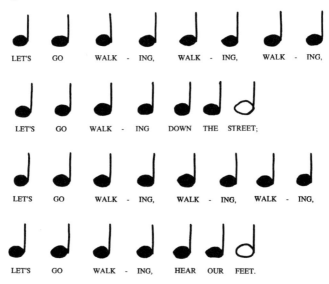

After the chant has been learned, the director can show the notes above the words on a blackboard and teach the children the kind of notes in music that tell us either to make the words "walk" or to slow down and "stroll." At future rehearsals review can be given by having just these note values placed on the board and the group asked to say the chant while different children take turns in pointing to the notes. This same procedure can also be employed for songs that the children have already learned by rote. The director can place just the note values of a familiar song on the board, and the children identify the song through its rhythmic association.

Eighth notes can be taught by first associating them with the physical activity of running. The following is a simple chant that is helpful for giving the children their introduction to "running notes."

The same procedures discussed for the teaching of quarter and half notes should be used in the presentation of these note values as well.

Through the use of the physical response and association approach, primary age children should be able to respond to and recognize the following note values by the time they finish the Primary Choir:

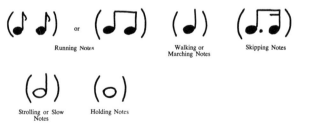

At each rehearsal the director can spend a few minutes in reviewing rhythm by having the children say correctly a rhythm pattern that has been placed on the blackboard. For example, the pattern could be shown as follows with different children taking turns in saying the rhythm words:

Impersonations and games can add much interest to rhythmic activities. The children can step like giants, warriors, elephants, horses, or run or skip like certain animals. In all of this, however, the creative approach is used; that is, the children themselves choose the type of response that they feel best interprets the music they hear or sing. This should lead them to the realization that different rhythms suggest different moods. Sometimes the music makes us feel like marching, running, or skipping, etc.; sometimes the music makes us feel happy, while at other times it makes us feel more sad, etc.

Further musical training for the Primary Choir should include an introduction to the basic elements of notation, such as the recognition of the treble and bass clef signs and the names of the lines and spaces in the treble clef. In introducing the names of the notes on the treble staff, it is good to begin with just the first three letters of the alphabet — A,B,C, and to learn thoroughly where these notes occur on the staff. After the children have mastered their "A,B,C's," in succeeding rehearsals they can be taught that only the first seven letters of their "school" alphabet are used in music and shown the lines and spaces above and below the "A,B,C's" they already know. A helpful technique for reviewing this information is the use of flash cards, which can be easily made or purchased from most music stores. Spelling games can also be used for this purpose. The children can be asked to show the positions of certain words containing the musical letters on a blackboard staff, etc. Primary children can also be taught the first five notes of a scale. This can be introduced by having the children sing — 1,2,3,4,5, or by improvising little words to the scale tune such as "watch me climb the scale," etc. Further training can include giving various children the experience of playing these five tones on the piano and, still later, of notating these notes on the staff.

In addition to some form of rhythm activity and theory work for each rehearsal, it is also helpful in developing musical concepts in primary children to include some listening to records. A director should begin to build his own library of records that are appropriate and of interest to children. A copy of the RCA Victor Educational Record Catalog will lend valuable assistance in this matter. For example, Victor E 104 is a fine recording of the various instruments in the orchestra. The Children's Record Club of the Month also has some fine records for use with younger children. Most of these records include lessons in appreciation, rhythm and singing all on a graded level. From time to time, a director can play various types of good sacred music: hymns, gospel songs, portions of oratorios, etc. A director should also encourage the children to listen to good sacred recordings at home and should advise them of the worth-while radio and television music programs.

Some general suggestions for teaching music listening and appreciation are listed briefly as follows:

1. Avoid bad recordings or poor equipment.
2. Show a keen interest yourself when playing the record.
3. Have definite objectives in mind for each listening activity. Give the group something definite to listen for — various instruments; various moods in the music; various activities suggested by the music, etc.
4. When there is a story to the music, don't tell the whole story at once or introduce too many details at one time. Maintain the children's interest by telling the story as you play the record.

Since the children have an acquaintance with reading at this age, the director can facilitate learning by putting clearly printed words of songs on the blackboard. Appropriate hymns of the church make excellent songs for primaries to learn this way. Song books and music sheets are still rather awkward and impractical for primaries to use consistently. Since this is an age when friends mean a great deal to the child, it is good to choose songs that speak of Jesus as a Friend and songs that tell how God loves children and wants to help them. God should never be pictured as One who is always watching children and waiting to punish them as soon as they misbehave.

It should be mentioned that this is the ideal age for a child to begin piano lessons. All music educators agree that the piano is the proper musical instrument on which any child should begin his musical training. At least a practical knowledge of piano will do much to give a foundation in music for future musical activity as well as life-long enjoyment. A church music director can do much to encourage his youngsters in this direction.

Some of the various collections useful for children of this age are: *Hymns for Primary Worship* by Curry, The Westminster Press; *Father, Hear Thy Children Sing*, Hall and McCreary Co.; *Primary Sing*, Scripture Press; *New Carols and Songs for Children* by Grimes, Carl Fisher.

Suggested names for a Primary Choir are: Carol Choir, Carillon Choir, Melody Choir.

JUNIOR CHOIRS

The Junior Choir is for boys and girls nine through twelve years of age or in the fourth, fifth, sixth and seventh grades. It should be mentioned, however, that it is not at all uncommon to have some twelve-year-old boys whose voices are beginning to experience a change. It generally is not wise to keep boys whose voices have reached a rather advanced stage of change with the unchanged voices. When this occurs, these boys should be placed in the Intermediate Choir.

The junior age is the peak of childhood. Juniors have reached a stage of physical and mental development which makes them capable of satisfying achievements. At this age their bodily and muscular co-ordination is well developed. The voice itself reaches its highest point of development during these years. The learning processes of the junior age child are much more developed than those of the primary age child. This is the age when the ability to memorize is at its peak. This fact combined with the longer span of attention and greater fluency of reading makes junior age the ideal time to emphasize a concentrated study of note reading.

It should be mentioned that this is the age when youngsters like to hold music in their hands as such an activity gives them a feeling of maturity. In addition this will aid them in their learning to read music. Junior age is also the ideal time to teach them hymn appreciation as well as the proper care of their church hymnal.

The following is a suggested procedure for teaching a new song by note rather than by rote. (This is assuming, however, that the proper preparatory work has been done at the earlier levels. If this is not the case, the director must first adapt the necessary readiness work suggested for the Primary Choir to the junior level before attempting this type of music reading program.)

1. Give the motivation for the song.
2. Explain any words that might be difficult to understand.
3. Look for any phrases or sections of the song that are identical or similar.
4. Study the rhythm of the song with the choir. Then have them clap or chant the words in rhythm.
5. Theory study of the song. Have the children find and sing the tonic chord notes for the key of this song (the do, mi, sol, or the 1, 3, 5). Have the scale of this song written on the blackboard and do review work on this. Have children tell on which note of the chord the song begins, ends, etc. Have children give the letter names of the notes, etc.
6. Match the words and rhythm with the melody. Play the song in its entirety with a strong stress on the melody and rhythm of the song. This can be made into a game (children at this age love games) by stopping on various notes and having the children tell the word or name the note where the music stopped, or they could hum back the phrase that has just been played, etc.
7. Have the children sing the song on a neutral syllable – i.e. "loo." Correct any wrong melodic or rhythmic tendencies. If the song is rather difficult, go back and study and sing each phrase separately.
8. Sing the song through in its entirety with the words.
9. If the interest is still high, sing another verse of the song, or begin working on the second part, etc., especially for those who need the added challenge for maintaining their interest.
10. Review again at the next rehearsal.

There are other musical areas where a director can realize definite developments for this age group. Correct concepts of singing can be continued at this age level. Juniors will take quite an interest in the matter of learning that each word as well as each syllable of each word is composed of vowel and consonant sounds. These children will take a real interest in producing and sustaining a tone with as clear and beautiful a vowel sound as possible. Such simple songs as the spiritual "Lord, I Want to Be a Christian" or "Near to the Heart of God" are excellent for this purpose. Phrasing, good bodily support, and effective interpretation can also be taught at this age.

One common type of incorrect tone quality among juniors is found in the boy who pitches his voice an octave lower than the correct unchanged quality range. Oftentimes this is purposeful, since a boy feels that he wants to sing like a man, especially if the director is a man. Boys must be taught that their voices will eventually change to a lower range and a heavier quality, but that until that time, they are causing harm to their voices by forcing themselves into a lower voice register. However, it may be possible that some of the twelve-year-old boys are beginning to experience a voice change and must be handled accordingly. During the early stages of their voice change they can be placed on the Second or Alto part, providing this part doesn't get too high. This problem of the changing voice is discussed in more detail in the next chapter. Another common fault is that children often sing too loudly, resulting in a forced, strident tone quality. Basically, children at this age love beauty, and with the right approach, this can make for the strongest appeal in the performance of songs.

In the Junior Choir most of the theory work should be in the form of review of the basic elements of music — names of lines and spaces in the treble clef, etc., all of which is geared to expedite the child's ability to read music. Learning to read music can and should be a great deal of fun for these keen youngsters. It should not be long before the majority of the junior children are able to clap the rhythms of new songs as well as to sight read with fair facility some of the easier ones. A helpful technique in giving these children further rhythm consciousness is to teach them the basic conducting patterns. Juniors take quite a delight in knowing these patterns and in directing the rest of the group from time to time. With the rhythm readiness work as well as an understanding of fractions which they have learned in their school studies, these children are able to be taught the relative relationships of note values. For example, walking notes are now known as quarter notes, running notes as eighth notes, etc. The arithmetical relationships of these notes can be taught by showing a circle on the blackboard representing the whole note and then dividing this into various sections with each section represented by its corresponding note value and rest. Following an understanding of the relative relationships of note values, these children can then be taught the meaning of time signatures. They should be told that the top number tells them how many notes or the equivalent of the kind indicated by the bottom number will be needed to fill any complete measure of music in that song. The bottom number is, then, merely another name for a note — i.e., 4 for quarter note, 2 for half note, 8 for eighth note, 1 for whole note, etc., identifying the kind of note that gets one of the beats in each of the measures. Through the use of the conducting patterns, the children can realize the meaning of "beat" as well as the fact that the first beat after each bar line is always the accented or "downbeat" in each measure. These children should also be taught that the letter "C," indicating Common Time, is oftentimes used in the time signature instead of the 4/4 time indication.

Further theory training for the Junior Choir should include the building of the complete scale. This should be started by showing the children the difference between half steps and whole steps on the keyboard. Practice should also be given in having them move their voices up or down half or whole steps from any given pitch. The children are then taught that to build a scale from any note there must be a whole step between every note except between the third and fourth notes and between the seventh and eighth notes of the scale, which will always have just a half step. After the children have participated in such activities as singing scales either with the numbers or by do, mi, sol, etc., or in having a turn to play a scale on the keyboard, or even on a toy marimba or filled glasses of water, they should be shown how to build a scale on the staff starting from any note. Following this introduction to scales and keys, concentrated study should be started to have them memorize the names and the accidentals of at least the first four sharp and flat keys as well as the key of C. Following a grasp of scale building, a study of intervals can be started. A useful technique for this is to play a game in the rehearsal using a "human scale or marimba." Eight children can be lined up and after they have sung a scale from a stated pitch, the number one child can sing his pitch and then call for a number to see if that child can sing his number and pitch quickly. By the time a child leaves the Junior Choir he should be able to sing a tonic chord from any pitch — the 1,3,5 notes of a scale, as well as any interval such as a third, fourth, etc., quickly and accurately. Junior age children should also be taught the names of the lines and spaces in the bass clef before completing the Junior Choir program. This is especially needful for the boys with changing voices who will be singing with the Intermediate Choir in the near future.

During the Junior Choir program the children should also be introduced to more complicated rhythm patterns. This would include:

1. The dotted quarter and eighth
2. The dotted eighth and sixteenth

3. The dotted half note
4. 6/8 meter with a two beat lilt to each measure
5. 9/8 meter with a three beat lilt to each measure
6. The triplet figure

Again, for each of these problems, the child must first of all know rote songs or have physical sensations that can be associated with the new problems he faces. For example, the dotted quarter and eighth can be associated with a familiar song such as "My Country, 'Tis of Thee," which the child already knows by rote.

Example

MY COUN - TRY 'TIS OF THEE - - - - etc.

It should again be mentioned that at this point no attempt should be made to teach the mathematical value of the dot (one half of the time value of the note it follows). After a sufficient background in the response and association approach, the intellectual understanding will follow naturally.

The dotted eighth and sixteenth rhythmic figure, previously introduced with the physical response of skipping, can now be shown and associated with a familiar song such as "Standing on the Promises."

Example

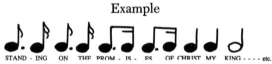

STAND - ING ON THE PROM - IS - ES OF CHRIST MY KING - - - - etc.

In introducing the dotted half note, it is not necessary nor wise to make a mathematical study of the meaning of the dot. Through a rhythm activity such as the conducting patterns, the children will begin to recognize the half note as a two-beat note and the dotted half as a three-beat note and will naturally assume that the dot is responsible for the extra beat. Later on, when further questions are asked, the director can give the technical explanation more fully.

In teaching a concept of 6/8 rhythm with a two-beat lilt to the measure, a director can put a chant such as "Humpty Dumpty" on a blackboard, showing the youngsters the value of these notes when taken in a "lilty" rhythm. A helpful gospel song that can be taught first by rote and then used as a basis for associational purposes in future learning is "Wonderful Words of Life."

Example

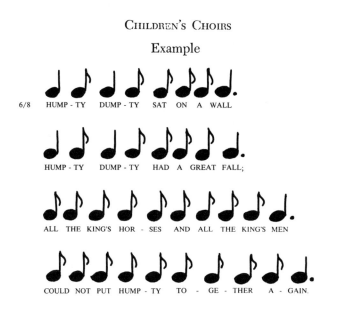

The 9/8 concept of a three-beat lilt to each measure can first be taught by teaching by rote the song "Blessed Assurance." Again, the use of the conductor's patterns for both the six and nine rhythm meters will help to give these youngsters this rhythmic concept of three pulsations to each main beat.

The triplet figure is generally associated with "gal-lop-ing notes." This could be illustrated on the blackboard as follows:

Example

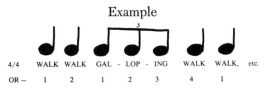

A Junior Choir rehearsal should also continue the activity of listening to records that was begun in the earlier age groups. Listening and studying the recordings of other good children's choirs can be especially interesting and helpful for one's own choir in developing a better level of interest and performance.

Another activity that many directors find useful for the junior age is the making of individual notebooks. Each child should have his own notebook cover to contain the individual pages for his book. This notebook would include any information that the director feels is pertinent for his particular group It is likely to include the following:

1. The name, address, telephone number, birthday and robe size of the child.
2. The rules of the group, its system of awards, points, etc.
3. Information regarding the care of robes, music, etc.
4. The words of a song to be memorized — i.e., the song the choir is singing at its next performance.
5. Music theory material that the choir might be studying: note values, clefs, names of notes, time signatures, key signatures, etc.
6. The words and meaning of the various congregational parts of the church service — Doxology, Gloria Patri, Offertory, Benediction, etc.
7. Outside work to be done on some aspect of music — special reports, pictures, etc.
8. Suggested Bible readings, Scripture verses to be learned, prayers for meal time, recordings for home use, radio or television programs of worth, etc.
9. Hymn appreciation material — stories of various hymns, etc. Good source books for this are *101 Hymn Stories* and *110 More Hymn Stories* by K. Osbeck, Kregel Publications.
10. Any special suggestions or instructions the director desires to send home to the parents.

An award system based on faithfulness and attitude can be an effective means of stimulating interest for the juniors. An appropriate award, such as a choir pin or bar, a certificate, a free time at camp, etc., presented at a special recognition service at the end of the season will do a great deal in establishing group pride and enthusiasm for the next season. This point system can be based on the following:

1. Attendance at rehearsals and performances.
2. Promptness at rehearsals and performances.
3. Behavior in rehearsal and in the services.
4. Memorizing the song to be performed.
5. Completing the notebook assignments.
6. Attending a musical concert or program.
7. Taking private music lessons.
8. Participating in some musical group at school.
9. Attendance at regular church services, Sunday school, youth group meetings, etc.
10. Some particular emphasis the director desires to make.

The task of recording these points is generally the responsibility of one of the choir mothers or sponsors. It may also be necessary for the director to give demerits for the sake of discipline. [1]

Using the various activities and techniques discussed in this chapter, a one hour rehearsal for Junior Choirs can be arranged as follows:

1. Theme Song — one that begins the rehearsal right on the stated time.
2. Greeting by the director.
3. Singing a song from memory that is well-known and well-liked.
4. Teaching a new rote song, chorus, or hymn of the month.
5. Theory work — work from the blackboard; various ways of studying a new song, etc.
6. Teaching and working on a new song by note.
7. Playing a musical game, or having some fun activity.
8. Working on a two part round, song, etc.
9. Listening time.
10. Notebook work.*
11. Discussing any group business — reminders, points and awards, socials, etc.
12. Singing several of the group's favorite songs.
13. Reviewing the song to be sung at the next service, possibly from the church sanctuary. Reviewing of seating or standing plans, how to march, etc.
14. Devotions and prayer.

The following suggestions are offered for having a successful rehearsal:

1. Know in advance what you want to accomplish in each rehearsal.
2. Arrive 20-30 minutes before rehearsal time. Have everything in readiness when children arrive — blackboard work, phonograph, chairs, etc.
3. Make atmosphere of the room attractive and interesting. Use a bulletin board, little displays, etc.
4. Greet each child cheerfully as he arrives. Invite him to remove outer garments, etc.
5. Have a planned pre-rehearsal activity when it is necessary for certain children to arrive early. These activities could include listening to special records, games, reading special articles or books on music, looking at display materials, working on notebooks, memory work, etc. This pre-rehearsal

---

*The author's book entitled *My Music Workbook* (Grand Rapids: Kregel Publications, 1971) completely develops this program.

activity can be the responsibility of the choir mothers or sponsors.

6. Have a theme song or special signal that begins the rehearsal right on time. End the rehearsal on time as well.

7. Have regular seats assigned for the rehearsal.

8. Begin the rehearsal with a song that is one of the children's favorites. End the rehearsal with a song that the children can sing well.

9. Don't rehearse too long on each number or stay too long on any activity. The entire rehearsal must have much variety and change of pace.

10. Begin each new instruction by reviewing what was taught at the previous rehearsal. Make new explanations clear and simple.

11. Don't show your displeasure with musical mistakes. Make corrections cheerfully. Give a lot of praise for any improvement.

12. Don't introduce the accompaniment to a song until the voice parts are well learned.

13. Don't be afraid to have fun with the group. Take time to play games such as "Simon Says," or to sing fun songs, or just to chat informally with the group regarding future plans, etc.

14. Be systematic regarding any group business, the keeping of attendance records, the enforcement of rules, etc.

15. Be the children's friend but don't become "palsy-walsy" with them. Speak in terms that they understand but never give the slightest impression that you are talking down to them.

16. Give a spiritual emphasis to the choir program. Conclude each rehearsal with a brief devotional challenge and with prayer.

17. Evaluate and analyze the results of each rehearsal.

Since the children of junior age are becoming quite social minded, two or three well planned social events throughout the year can do a great deal in developing group enthusiasm and prestige. The end of the choir year is an ideal time for a major social. This could include a picnic, skating or swimming party, a trip, etc. Plans for a group picture or a recording at the close of the season always stimulate interest. Many churches have developed excellent interest in the junior age group by combining the activities of the church's youth work with the choir rehearsal.

For example, the juniors could be invited to the church right after school, have a recreation, craft and Bible study under the direction of the pastor or youth leader, attend a choir rehearsal, and still be home in time for dinner.

The spiritual content of the songs that a director chooses for the junior age group is especially important. This is the age when children can fully understand what it means to accept Christ as their personal Saviour, as well as to dedicate their lives to God's glory. Songs of salvation, praise, service and devotion should predominate. This is an ideal time to teach the great hymns of the church which speak of worship, prayer, stewardship, as well as the other areas of the Christian life. Far too many of our evangelical churches give these keen youngsters nothing but the lighter songs and choruses, with the result that many never develop any real musical as well as spiritual depth and maturity.

A church music director can do much to encourage his junior age youngsters to further their musical training and enjoyment beyond their choir experience. Those taking piano lessons should be encouraged to continue their lessons. Whenever possible, these children, when they become proficient, should be used for various church occasions. Those who have not yet started piano lessons should be encouraged to begin as soon as possible. This is also the ideal time for these youngsters to begin an orchestral instrument, as this will give them countless hours of personal pleasure during their future schooling as well as in the church program.

Suggested names for a Junior Choir are: Carol Choir, Crusader Choir, Sunshine Chorus.

MATERIALS AND HELPS

Since there is such an abundance of good materials for Junior Choirs, only a brief listing of various collections is made here. A list of individual octavo numbers can be obtained from most publishing houses.

1. *A Junior's Praise*, by Osbeck. Published by Kregels.
2. *Let Youth Praise Him*. Published by Eerdmans.
3. *Hymns for Junior Worship*. Published by Westminster Press.
4. *Our Songs of Praise*. Published by Concordia.
5. Quarterly magazines for both Primary and Junior Choirs available from The Sunday School Board of the Southern Baptist Convention, 127 Ninth Ave. North, Nashville, TN

37234. Includes interesting stories and activities with sea-
sonal music and demonstration record.

6. *Music for Children* — A comprehensive music education program for the entire graded choir curriculum. Published by
David C. Cook.

7. *The Alleluia Series.* A coordinated two year program of worship, music and arts for children. Published by the Augsburg Publishing House.

From time to time the Junior Choir program can be greatly
encouraged by combining the Junior and Senior Choirs for special
occasions such as Christmas and Easter. It is especially effective
to use songs that employ the Junior Choir as a descant or obligato
to the Senior Choir voice parts. Most publishing houses have a
good supply of numbers of this type and will supply approval
copies upon request.

PART SINGING

With the proper amount of background in rote singing, theory,
rhythm work, ear training and sight reading, two-part singing can
be introduced at the junior age level once the choir program is
well established. The initial approach should be that of training
the ear and developing singing independence rather than mere
drill on each part. It is an established fact that the ear must be
trained to hear harmony first before it can be read. Also, it is
wise at first not to designate voices as either soprano or alto. Rather,
until about the time of the sixth grade, simply divide the choir by
Part I and Part II with everyone getting experience in singing a
harmony part. In choirs where there are only sixth and seventh
graders, even three-part music may eventually be used. A suggested procedure for developing part singing in a Junior Choir is
listed as follows:

1. Use songs with a good piano accompaniment to establish
the sound of harmony.

2. Use songs with an instrumental obligato part. This is good
practice for the youngster who plays the instrument as well
as good training for the group in hearing a harmony part
while they are singing.

3. The director or another adult can sing a harmony part while
the choir sings the melody.

4. Use songs and choruses by rote that employ a simple round
or descant. For example, the following chorus sung to the

tune of "Sweet Choral Bells" in the key of C makes an excellent two-part round:

"Only one life and it will soon be past;
Only what is done for Jesus Christ will last."

Such books as *Rounds and Canons* by Wilson, published by Hall and McCreary, *Our First Songs with Descants* and *Songs to Sing with Descants*, both by Krone and published by Kjos, are helpful for this purpose.

5. Teach songs that have a second part that is very melodic — one that can be learned as "another melody" to the song.

6. Begin a concentrated program of two part reading using the same procedures as those employed in unison reading, only doing the two part reading simultaneously as much as possible.

7. Gradually begin using songs where the second part is more of a regular alto or harmony part.

MONOTONISM

One of the rather difficult problems that confront directors of children's choirs is the problem of monotonism. In the majority of cases the non-singing child will find his singing voice naturally himself merely by having the opportunity to sing, especially if he is introduced to music and learns to enjoy it at an early age such as in the Beginner or Primary Choir programs. There are, however, numerous cases of children who need more specialized help in this matter.

There are a number of possible causes for monotonism. One of the most prevalent is a limited musical background in the home. The child has just never been encouraged to hear or experience much music. It is possible, however, that a non-singing child has some physical difficulty. This could include such defects as the lack of normal bodily co-ordination, defective hearing, diseased throat, adenoids or nose.

Most generally, though, the basic cause of monotonism is a psychological one. It might be a lack of concentration by a nervous or neurotic child or some complex that a child has developed about singing due to an embarrassment it has caused him in the past. Generally speaking, most non-singing children are suffering from some form of self-consciousness and inhibition.

Since monotonism is, then, so often associated with the psychological make-up of the child, one of the first things a director must do is to establish the proper rapport between himself and the child.

The director should treat the matter in a sincere, matter-of-fact manner. The child must learn to have complete confidence in the fact that the director is his friend in helping him with his singing problem, rather than someone who will add to his embarrassment. One of the most important things a director can do for the child at this stage is to win his confidence and to develop his desire and will to find his singing voice.

It should be of encouragement to directors to note that music educators in general agree that there is no such thing as a hopeless monotone, and that with the exception of extreme physical and psychological handicaps, every child will respond to treatment. Once the director has gained the child's confidence and has developed his will to sing, there are several sound techniques that can be used. For the most part, all of these techniques are concerned with helping the child find his head or upper tone quality. Often there are children who are partial monotones or who are able to sing several tones on pitch as long as they sing them with their "chesty" quality. These children lose all concept of pitch, however, as soon as a song gets into their upper registers.

For younger children the tone matching games discussed previously in connection with the Beginners' Choir are excellent. With a little imagination these can be a great deal of fun and help for the child. Another technique is that of associating a physical sensation with the singing voice. For example, a stairway can be used and as the child ascends or descends he sings the numbers 1,2,3,4,5, etc., or 5,4,3,2,1. Sometimes just a slight lifting of the child will help him get this up and down concept with his voice.

What many directors like to do is simply to have an "extra special session" or a training rehearsal of just the non-singing children in an informal session for fifteen minutes or so before or after the regular rehearsal. Here in a small group around the keyboard, with everyone experiencing the same problem, effective help can be given without causing individual embarrassment. A child can be asked to make any singing sound that he can. On the piano the director can then show the child the note just sung. The director can then show him that the next note to the right or left would mean that his voice too would have to go up or down just a little. Gradually larger jumps can be made at the keyboard and with the child's voice. Within a relatively few sessions of this type, the child will begin experiencing his singing voice. Soon little well-known tunes such as "Mary Had a Little Lamb," "Jesus Loves Me," etc., can be sung as well as played with one finger at the keyboard.

Once this step is gained, it isn't long before the non-singing child is able to take his regular place as a worthy choir member. It may be necessary for a time, however, to have these children seated so that the exceptionally strong singers are placed behind and around them.

Again it should be emphasized that the main approach in helping monotones is to establish confidence in their own singing ability in a patient, helpful manner. Never should a director show the slightest displeasure with these children by placing them in another part of the room and telling them to listen while the rest of the choir sings. Never should a non-singing child be corrected before the entire group. Directors who employ the technique of having the non-singing children merely mouth the words during a performance while the choir is singing should be completely aware of the possible psychological danger of this practice to the child. It is our personal conviction that no individual performance is nearly as important as the possible harm that can be caused a young child.

STARTING A CHILDREN'S CHOIR

The following suggestions are offered for starting and promoting a new children's choir in a church. Foremost, obtain the approval and support of the pastor, church board and music committee for such an endeavor. It is also wise to enlist the cooperation of several key mothers and fathers who are especially interested and concerned about such a project. This can be followed by a survey of the potential children in the various departments of the Sunday school from which the children will be drawn. About three weeks should be allowed for promotional work before the first rehearsal is announced. During this time verbal announcements can be given in the church services and in the Sunday school sessions, with letters or cards sent to the various homes.

At the first rehearsal parents should be invited to attend with their children. At this meeting both parents and children can be impressed with the objectives and responsibilities of the choir program. Some directors use pledge cards at this session that are passed out and signed by both parents and children, pledging their faithful attendance and support of the choir. Often directors include brief voice tests at this time. This can either be done individually or in small groups of children. This gives the director a quick survey of the talent and guides him in his choice of music. It also helps him to spot the non-singing children so that he can make plans to give them special attention. It should be mentioned, however, that these voice tests are never given for the purpose of eliminating anyone from the choir program. Following several weeks of faithful attendance, each child can be given a membership card entitling him to remain permanently with the choir and to receive his robe.

DISCIPLINE

Disciplinary problems and weak control of children's choirs are caused most frequently by a lack of real preparation and genuine enthusiasm on the part of the leader. Most discipline problems will automatically take care of themselves with plenty of well-planned, interesting activities.

A good children's leader is one who combines strength with tenderness. A child must realize that the leader is absolutely fair and sincere even in matters of reprimand. Children basically want to sense that a leader is in absolute control of every situation. To permit a child to do whatever he pleases is to remove the basic securities that are necessary for his growth, development and maturity. When these restraints are wise and firm, they become a source of stability rather than a source of irritation and unrest.

The following suggestions are offered regarding discipline:

1. Take time to know each child personally.
2. Keep a balance between genuine friendliness and mature dignity.
3. Don't talk down to children or speak in a pedantic manner.
4. Use praise much more than scolding.
5. Never use ridicule or sarcasm as a means of discipline.
6. Don't try to outshout the children. Don't talk as long as anyone else is talking. Speak with a low, confident tone when leading.
7. Be aware of the possible causes of disciplinary problems:
   a. The weather — gloomy, rainy days cause much more restlessness than do bright, sunny days.
   b. Misdirected energy.
   c. Resentment of control on the part of a "spoiled child."
   d. Distractions in the rooms.
   e. Imitators of other children.
   f. Those desiring special attention and affection.
   g. Inadequate facilities: improper lighting, heating, ventilation; not enough space for the games and rhythm activities; chairs that are not proper size for the children (their feet should always be able to touch the floor), etc.
   h. Limited mental and physiological abilities.

8. Work in close cooperation with the parents.
9. Remember, as long as you the director are in control of yourself, you can control any situation that might arise.
10. Bear in mind that in your leadership you are not alone, but have the aid and strength that the Spirit of God will provide in times of emergency and need.

CHOIR MOTHERS AND SPONSORS

To administer a complete music program in a church, a music director will need the cooperation of a large number of people. Foremost will be the wholehearted cooperation of the pastor and music committee. However, for the children's choirs, one of the most important groups in assisting the director can be the choir mothers and sponsors. These mothers and fathers can assist each choir in such matters as: the enlistment and enrollment of new members; notifying parents regarding choir policies; transportation problems; clerical work — attendance records, point system, etc.; pre-rehearsal activities; supervisory assistance during the church service performances; care of the robes; help for the social functions, etc. Needless to say, helpers for matters such as these can provide invaluable assistance for the director. A director should generally plan to have one choir mother or sponsor for every seven or eight children.

ROBING CHILDREN'S CHOIRS

Almost every choir leader will agree that there are real benefits in vesting all of the various choirs in the church. To mention just a few of these benefits: robes give dignity and richness to a church service; robes minimize the individual, placing the rich and the poor on the same basis; robes give a unity to a group of individuals; robes lend prestige to the group; and, especially with children, the director can make the issuing of a robe a meaningful experience. However, the cost of vesting several choirs is generally quite a financial undertaking for most churches. Commercial robes for children's choirs will usually range in price from $25.00 to $30.00 each. This cost generally necessitates that most churches make their own robes.

Robing can be as simple or as elaborate as desired. For example, a children's choir can be robed by simply cutting out of stiff paper or cotton cloth a simple cape that fits over the head. Another possibility might be a simple bolero vest, worn over white shirts and blouses and tied around the neck with a big bow. Several of the more elaborate patterns for children's choir robes are those shown by McCall's, model numbers 689 and 1957, and the Butterick pattern, number 6596. There is also a Vestment Cutout Kit sold by S. Theodore Cuthbertson, Inc., 2013 Samson St., Philadelphia, with all of the vestments cut out and packaged, with easy to follow sewing instructions. Both McCall's and Butterick patterns can be used as a basis for making different robes for the various children's choirs. For example, for the Beginner's Choir, a single piece, fingertip length cotta could be adapted, with special ties that could be pinned on. The Primary Choir could have much the same idea with perhaps a variation in color or with a different type of bow. For the juniors, a two piece idea of cotta and skirt adds smartness.

There are several other considerations that one should keep in mind regarding robes. All of the robes should harmonize with each other as well as with the carpets and furnishings in the sanctuary. It is generally best if the robe provides light color next to the child's face. Robes with too light a color generally will not be practical since they will show dirt too easily and require a great deal of dry cleaning. The collars or bibs usually add enough of the lighter and contrasting color to the darker color of the skirt or cotta. Robes must be easy for the child to get into quickly before the service. In this regard, children must be taught proper care of their individual robes. This means that all robes must be hung after each use and stored where they can be covered and free from dust and fumes. The added accessories, such as collars, bows, stoles, should be stored separately without folding.

MISCELLANEOUS SUGGESTIONS

The following are miscellaneous suggestions regarding children's choirs:

1. A competent pianist is an absolute necessity for all of the children's choirs. Just anyone will not do. The accompanist should stress the melody, steady rhythm and lightness of style rather than the heavier, congregational style of playing which emphasizes full harmonies, strong bass, ornamental notes, etc.

2. Do not have too wide an age range in any group. If a church can have only two children's choirs, it would be best to have one group of children from age 5 through 7 and another group from age 8 through 12. If a church can have only one choir, it would be best to begin with the 8,9,10,11,12 year age group and to lend whatever assistance

possible to Sunday school teachers, etc., in the way of appropriate materials and suggestions for their work with the younger children.

3. Plan the entire year's work in advance, preferably in the summer. Build the schedule first around the special days of the year — Thanksgiving, Christmas, Easter, Mother's Day, Recognition Sunday, etc., and then fill in other times that are possible. On an average, a Junior Choir director should allow himself at least four rehearsals for each performance. A director should make every effort to have the children memorize their music for each performance. In the rehearsals immediately preceding the performance, a director must allow enough time to practice the mechanics of a performance — how to march, where to sit or stand, etc., so that these mechanics are thoroughly impressed in each child's mind. Generally, a child who misses these instructions should not be allowed to sing for the service.

4. Scheduling a rehearsal time is always a problem. Most rehearsals are generally held after school or on Saturday morning. Occasionally some churches schedule the rehearsal after the evening dinner hour, Sunday afternoon, as part of the mid-week or family night service, or possibly before the Sunday evening service. There is also the possibility of having a rehearsal as part of the Sunday school, junior church, or the youth group meeting. If at all possible, however, avoid conflicts with other church activities.

5. If at all possible, try to obtain some and eventually all of the following:

   A basic set of rhythm instruments, a set of resonator bells, an autoharp, possibly song flutes — tonnettes or recorders for each member, a record player with good fidelity, a hymnal geared for children, a blackboard with staff lines, a piano in good tune, workbooks and quarterly music magazines.

6. For directors who like to include choral reading work with children's choirs, a good book for reference for this purpose is *Choral Reading for Worship and Inspiration* by Brown and Heltman, Published by Westminster Press.

7. A children's choir will enjoy working on a mini-drama production to close the season. Many fine works have been published in recent years.

8. Conclude the season by having a picture taken of the group. Also a special recognition night for those who have been faithful members throughout the year.

ASSIGNMENTS

1. Give at least five important reasons for having a graded children's choir program in the local church.
2. Why is it important that the choir experience include every child and not just the obviously talented? Why is it so important that the non-singing child be given special help and attention? What psychological harm can be done in having the non-singing children merely listen or perhaps mouth the words during a performance? As a director, if a choice has to be made between a quality performance and psychologically injuring a non-singing child, what would be your choice?
3. Prepare a typical 25-30 minute rehearsal plan for a Primary Choir. Show all of the various activities to be included and the time to be spent on each.
4. Prepare a typical 45-60 minute rehearsal plan for a Junior Choir. Show all of the activities to be included and the time to be spent on each.
5. Discuss ways in which discipline problems can be avoided or lessened by proper planning and management in a rehearsal.

ADDITIONAL READING

1. *Guiding the Primary Child.* Published by Broadman Press.
2. *How to Teach Children Music* by Stinson. Published by Harper Company.
3. *Leading Children's Choirs* by Sample. Published by Broadman Press.
4. *Organizing and Directing Children's Choirs* by Ingram. Published by Abingdon Press.
5. *The Children's Choir* by Jacobs, Vols. 1 and 2. Published by Augustana Press.

5 | INTERMEDIATE — TEEN-AGE — YOUNG PEOPLE'S CHOIRS

The Intermediate Choir or the age group from the ages of thirteen through high school is generally considered the most difficult of all church choirs for any director to administer. The adolescent personality combined with various difficult musical problems present a real challenge for any director.

Beginning and Promoting the Choir

When beginning an Intermediate Choir to span the gap between the Junior and Senior Choirs, it generally is best to have just one choir for the whole thirteen through high school age span. (This might possibly include some twelve-year-old boys whose voices are changing.) If this choir grows beyond its most efficient size, or if there develops too great a problem with the younger boys and their changing voices, or if social conflicts develop between the older and younger members, it will be necessary to divide the group, starting from twelve or thirteen years to or through fifteen years of age, with another choir for the remainder of the high school age. The first choir would represent the junior high school age group while the latter choir would represent the senior high school age level.

Since teen-agers are especially aware of and concerned with the approval of their friends, it is important when starting an Intermediate Choir to get first the key young people in the Sunday school classes or youth department sold on the idea of a choir program just for them. In the initial promotion it should be stressed that this choir will be open to all young people of the church as well as their friends regardless of individual musical ability. This, then, can be an excellent evangelistic endeavor in attracting non-Christian teen-agers into the group and in so doing bringing them under the influence of the church. In addition to having the enthusiastic support of the pastor, youth leaders, Sunday school teachers, etc., it is also necessary when starting an Intermediate Choir to contact the parents individually to gain their cooperation in encouraging the faithfulness of their young people for the choir program.

THE JUNIOR HIGH LEVEL

The junior high school age is in particular an age of turmoil. The physical changes which take place during early adolescence are the cause of the many problems which accompany this period of life. Rapid physical growth and biological changes often are the cause of much self-consciousness. Emotionally, the adolescent finds himself face to face with problems which in previous years had no bearing on his life, namely the emergence and rapid development of sex feelings and impulses. Often there is a sense of frustration as the adolescent's intellectual maturity and his desire to lead an adult life are not compatible with his muscular coordination and emotional maturity. All of these changes and developments account for such traits as boisterousness, silliness, restlessness, day-dreaming, awkwardness, etc. Generally there are many individual differences as far as maturity is concerned. Especially is this true of girls, who are much more mature than the boys at this age level. The adolescent age is often an age when inferiority complexes develop, especially for those youngsters who mature more slowly than the rest of their group. Such young people often withdraw from the rest of the group and become sullen and unusually sensitive.

A choir director working with young adolescents must understand their physical and emotional problems and accept them as they are. He must cultivate a sincere attitude of friendliness, kindness and patience with them. Although there must be firmness and discipline, it must be a discipline with love. When impatience replaces love and a dominating attitude replaces friendship, the choir director has ceased being a real leader. He must take a keen interest in the teen-ager's school life, his personal problems and local interests if he is to gain his support and confidence.

A director's choice of songs is especially important in working with this age group. Although the junior high school age is an age of turmoil, it is also an age of decision. This is the ideal time to challenge the youngsters to make a personal acceptance of Jesus Christ as the Lord and Saviour of their lives. Although the music director does not want to be preaching all of the time, an occasional word as well as the songs that are chosen can do much to impress this vital truth upon the minds of the young people. The director should also use songs that emphasize the faith and confidence we can have in Christ as Christians if we trust our lives to Him for daily guidance.

THE CHANGING VOICE

One of the most difficult problems confronting a director of a junior high age choir is the peculiar problem of the changing voice. The process of change occurs with most boys between the ages of twelve and sixteen. After the adolescent voice has gone through its complete change, which may take from several weeks to several years, a boy's larynx and vocal chords have approximately doubled in length and in thickness. This doubling in length lowers the pitch of boys' voices approximately one octave. A girl's vocal chords during adolescence also experience a change; however, the pitch and quality changes are not nearly as great or drastic as those of a boy.

There are several characteristics that the alert director can detect to determine when the boys' voices begin to change. They are:

1. Unusual physical growth, heavier facial features, downy skin, enlarged "adam's apple," etc.
2. A speaking voice that becomes husky and heavier and lacking in control.
3. Often a brilliant treble quality just before the change occurs.

It is now generally agreed by most music educators that adolescent boys can continue singing even during the "break" if they are kept from straining or forcing the voice in any way. One of the chief vocal considerations when working with adolescents, then, is to be sure that they stay within their most comfortable singing ranges. Also, there is often a tendency for younger boys to try to be basses prematurely, while older boys sometimes sing with either a timid half voice, resulting in fuzzy tones, or attempt tones beyond their range by means of straining. All such poor singing habits must be discouraged. Rather than singing with this type of restricted throat and chest tone quality, singers of this as well as of all age groups must be taught the basic concepts of good tone production which are: body support, relaxed jaw and throat, forward tongue, and the development and blending of the upper register quality with the rest of one's voice.

Adolescent voices vary in range and ability but generally can be placed in one of these classifications:

Girl Sopranos or the
unchanged, high boys' voices

Girl Altos or the
unchanged, low boys' voices

Boys whose voices are in the
early stages of change

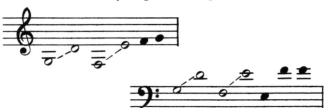

Boy baritones — a more
advanced stage of change

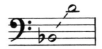

Changed tenors

Changed baritones or basses

The boy's voice in the early stages of change has several names. Some educators refer to it as the alto-tenor voice; others speak of it merely as tenor, while still others refer to it as the cambiata voice. Authorities vary on the actual singing ranges of these voices, opinions ranging from F below Middle C to anywhere to third space C on the treble staff. A range from G or F below Middle C to Middle C, D, or possibly Eb is considered a safe, average range. As a voice gradually changes, a boy should be assigned to a lower part. This whole matter of a boy's changing voice should be treated in such a natural, matter of fact manner by the director that it should be the normal experience for a boy to develop a natural curiosity about his own voice so that he will of his own initiative ask the director to test his voice occasionally to see how the change is progressing. Often the attitude develops with boys of this age that singing is "sissy." One helpful way of overcoming this type of thinking is to play recordings occasionally of outstanding men singers, boys' choruses, male choral groups, etc. When testing these changing boys' voices, a director should always vocalize on descending scales and chords, thus bringing their upper quality down rather than encouraging any strain of pushing the lower quality up. A voice part should always be one that a boy can sing easily and comfortably. Where there are unchanged boys' voices in the choir, these boys should be placed on the regular soprano or alto parts but allowed to sit with the rest of the boys.

It must be admitted that practical, sacred music that is geared for the junior high and early senior high school ages is limited both in quality and quantity. Some directors try to solve this problem by using regular SAB arrangements. This generally is not too satisfactory since these arrangements are made especially for adult voices, and the baritone parts are usually too demanding both harmonically and vocally for teen-age boys. More music that is especially arranged for early adolescent voices is definitely needed for the church music program.

As a result of this lack of music, I have found it necessary to make most of my own arrangements when working with teen-age choirs. Invariably these groups in their early stages have been limited both in size and in musical ability. Boys at this age have little concept of a tenor or bass harmony part; in fact, a director is quite fortunate if the majority of these boys can even carry a melody with reasonable accuracy. This experience has prompted me to prepare a collection of these arrangements for publication. These arrangements, *Teen-Age Praise*, have the following underlying features:

1. The use of appropriate, standard hymns and gospel songs whose message is geared to the spiritual needs of teen-agers.
2. Basically arranged in three parts with the boys' parts arranged in a voice range so that both the changing and changed voices sing the same part. This vocal range is generally in the C to middle C octave.
3. The boys' parts generally carry the melody of the song with the girls furnishing the harmony as interestingly as possible.
4. Cadence progressions in easy four-part style to give occasional practice in four-part singing.
5. A piano accompaniment that adds interest and fullness to the voice parts.

Once the group develops musically and as the changing voices begin to mature, one can gradually lead them into a better quality of SATB music.

The Senior High Level

The senior high school age is an age of vision and adventure. Here the young people are beginning to do some serious and individual thinking about their future plans. Spiritually, this age group is often filled with doubts regarding spiritual truths, with the result that there is generally a time of uncertainty and searching for ideals and standards of their own. Needless to say, a music director has a real opportunity to be of help to these young people when the right opportunities arise by encouraging them in the Christian faith and by facing their questions and doubts in an honest and frank manner. Although the moods, plans and ideals of these young people can be quite changeable, they generally have a great deal of aesthetic appreciation for beauty and the finer qualities of life. The music director should always be aware of choosing songs that speak of decision and determination to put God first in one's life and in so doing to know the meaning of a victorious Christian life. This is also the time to enlarge these young people's appreciation and understanding of the great hymns and other forms of sacred music and to instruct them in the meaning and practice of personal and corporate worship.

Once the changing voice stage is passed and the young people have gained some basic concepts of singing, the problem of choosing music for the high school or young people's choir is not too difficult. The possibilities for fine musical achievement by this age group are practically unlimited. Generally there is more danger in underestimating the abilities of these keen-minded young people than there is in over-taxing them. The director has a wealth of good sacred SATB music that will inspire and challenge this age group. Such a choir will enjoy singing numbers that employ a wide range of moods and styles, ranging from spirituals and hymn arrangements to all types of good anthems. However, it must be cautioned that real vocal harm can be done teen-age voices by having them sing demanding choral works intended for trained, mature voices, especially where these works employ extreme ranges for prolonged passages. The music chosen, then, must strike that happy balance of having sufficient musical difficulty to present a learning challenge and yet of not being beyond the vocal capabilities of the group.

It should also be mentioned that valuable encouragement and assistance can also be given the more interested and talented teen-agers in a church by organizing smaller ensembles such as girls' trios, sextettes, boys' quartets, mixed quartets, instrumental groups, etc. A vital music program for young people will do much to insure the success of a youth program in any church.

Rehearsal Techniques

The following suggestions are offered with respect to conducting a successful rehearsal for a teen-age choir. Generally, a rehearsal period should not be more than 45-50 minutes in length. Above all, the rehearsal time must be kept moving and interesting. Should the rehearsal become lax or uninteresting, the group will use the time as an excuse for frivolity. It should be cautioned that continuous frivolity with lack of leader control will eventually cause the individual members to lose interest in the group. It should also be mentioned that a fine accompanist is especially needful for this age group. An accompanist who plays in a stiff, mechanical and inaccurate manner will become the object of many "behind the back" jokes. The accompanist should also be sensitive to helping the various voice parts. For example, when a new song is being learned, the accompanist should play only the voice parts and be able to give special emphasis to the part that needs extra help. To control a group of teen-agers, then, there must be an enthusiastic and vital spirit in all phases of the leadership.

There are several definite DON'TS that a teen-age choir director should heed when conducting a rehearsal. These are listed briefly as follows:

1. Don't have your back to the group any longer than necessary.
2. Don't be stationary. Rather, be active. Move about the group helping whatever part needs help, etc.

3. Don't display emotional, personal feelings.
4. Don't reprimand individuals in front of the entire group.
5. Don't start or end rehearsals late. Rather, be businesslike about all group activities.
6. Never appear discouraged with the results. For example, never allow complete failure with any song. Don't let the rehearsal end poorly. Keep a positive, optimistic spirit about the group.
7. Don't have favorites.
8. Don't treat teen-agers as children.
9. Never show any awareness of any physical abnormality — voice control, skin blemishes, awkwardness, etc.
10. Don't make any statement you cannot fulfill.

A director must make every effort to plan his rehearsals thoroughly in advance. It is good to have more activity planned than can possibly be accomplished during the regular time. Although a director must "think through" his rehearsal in advance, he must be flexible enough to inject some new activity or new song whenever he senses that the interest is lagging. In arranging one's seating plan, it is wise to place the best singers behind those who need help. All physical preparation, such as room arrangement, music distribution and blackboard work, should always be done before the entire group assembles.

A sample rehearsal can be planned as follows:

1. Sing through from memory several well-known, well-liked choruses, hymns or gospel songs. This is for the purpose of warming up, attracting attention and establishing interest. However, be sure that these songs are pitched in the right vocal range for the fellows. It can also be helpful to have a mimeographed list of songs for this use.
2. Have a brief time of welcome, greeting, informal fun, etc.
3. Teach a new "sure-fire" chorus or song by rote.
4. Theory work. This can include a brief injection of musical knowledge such as rhythm patterns, key and time signatures, tonic chords, etc. It can also include having on a blackboard various chord progressions which are taken from one or more of the part songs to be sung. This provides an excellent opportunity for brief drills on various sight singing problems, emphasizing blend and sensitive listening on various vowel sounds, humming, etc. (Adolescent youngsters are enthusiastic hummers. Teach them to hum correctly — say the word "Hun" and very easily bring the lips together.)

5. Read through and study a new part song for future use. Whenever possible use a good recording of this number to introduce it to the choir.

6. Sing through and perfect the number to be sung at the next service. Use the piano/tape accompaniment, stress interpretation, tone quality, diction, phrasing, etc.

7. Review and drill briefly on just the places that contain a problem in a song that the choir has recently started.

8. Work on some long-range project — musicale, drama production, etc.

9. Sing from the choir loft the number to be sung at the next service. Work on the mechanics of performance — marching, sitting, uniformity of holding music, etc.

10. Close with some familiar, favorite part song or chorus. A discussion of any organizational business, a brief devotional challenge, prayer, etc.

Choir Organization

A teen-age choir, like most choir groups, should have its own plan of organization. This would include the necessary officers such as president, vice-president, secretary-treasurer, librarian, social chairman, robe chairman, etc. Such policies as the admission of new members, the collection and expenditures of finances, standards for rewarding faithfulness, planning of socials, etc., can all be the responsibility of the group, with, of course, the careful and tactful supervision of the director. The wise director will, then, let the rules and the enforcement of those rules be a group action rather than his own direct and strong-armed type of leadership.

Although most teen-agers like to pretend that they are extremely busy and have no time for any new activity, they generally respond quite readily to any social program. In some church youth programs it has proved extremely successful to make for this group a complete evening's program built around the choir rehearsal, with the assistance of the pastor and other youth leaders. For example, the program could begin at 5:45 P.M. with a supper at the church. This could be followed by the choir rehearsal, after which there could be a time of Bible study, recreation and fellowship. This type of activity can do a great deal in developing a strong youth organization within a church. The important matter of choosing the right time for such a program will, of course, have to be done with consideration of existing local community and church situations. In some churches it has proved successful to have the music program as part of the weekly prayer or family night service. Here, the young people could have their own group for Bible study, prayer, choir rehearsal, etc. Periodic socials such as roller or ice skating parties, picnics, hikes, hay or sleigh rides, Christmas carol sings, etc., will always do much toward establishing stronger loyalties for the choir. An occasional small treat such as a box of candy from the director will also do a great deal to further enthusiasm. As with the other choirs of the church, attractive and distinctive robes, especially attired with nice stoles or surplices, will add real prestige to such a group. Singing with the other choirs of the church for special occasions will also add interest. A distinctive name, such as the Choraleers, The Ambassadors, The Coronation Choir, The Harmony Chorus, The King's Heralds, The Chorale, The Chapel Choir, is also important in this respect.

Today, teen choirs are especially interested in performing contemporary musicales, dramatic productions, singing with sound tracks, etc. Many fine materials have been published in recent years. Broadman Press and the Lexicon Company have done a great deal in this area. Several of the more popular works include:

"Tell It Like It Is"   "Show Me"   "Decisions"   "Life"
"Hello"

Valuable encouragement and assistance can also be given the more interested and talented teenagers in a church by helping them with solo work, or by organizing smaller ensembles such as girls' trios, sextettes, boys' quartets, instrumental groups, gospel teams including drama-puppets-music, etc. These special groups can be used effectively not only within the church program but in an evangelistic outreach ministry as well.

Another musical activity especially geared for younger high school boys is the handbell choir. This activity has been successfully used in many churches in recent years. Although the financial involvement for a complete set of quality bells is a sizable investment for most churches, directors who have organized such groups and have experienced the enthusiastic response from these teens, generally agree that it is a worthy endeavor. Two helpful books on this subject are: *The Art of Handbell Ringing* by Nancy Poore Tuffs, published by Abingdon Press, and *Handbell Ringing in Church* by Ellen Jane Lorenz, published by the Lorenz Company.

CONCLUSIONS

Despite the problems and hard work involved in working with teen-agers, one must continually remind himself of the importance of this particular group. Not only is the musical development important as new members are groomed for the senior choir, but of far greater importance is the spiritual responsibility. This often is the age when spiritual convictions are either deepened or the young person is permanently attracted to interests outside of the church. It is often the case that a musical activity is the last interest a young person clings to in the church to tide him over till he reaches sounder spiritual maturity. This truth places a real challenge and responsibility upon any music director. However, to see young people commit their lives to God and to give themselves wholeheartedly to His service is a thrill that is worth many hours of toil and preparation.

The following is a brief list of collections and individual numbers that can be used with intermediate choirs:

1. *Teen-Age Praise* by Osbeck. Distributed by Kregels.
2. *Gospel Choir Classics*, Vol. I, II, III. Published by Zondervan.
3. *The Chapel Choir Book* by Perry. Published by Presser Co.
4. *Sing God's Praise* by Tkach. Published by Kjos Music Co.
5. *Young People's Choir* edited by Perry. Published by Presser Co.
6. *Anthems for the Youth Choir* edited by Curry. Published by Westminster Press.

INTERMEDIATE — TEEN-AGE — YOUNG PEOPLE'S CHOIRS

7. *Carols for Christmas* by Heller. Published by Hall & McCreary Co.
8. *Tunetime for Teentime* by Cooper. Published by Carl Fischer.
9. *The Singing Teens* by Cooper. Published by Gordon V. Thompson, Ltd.
10. *Cambiata Hymnal* by Cooper. Published by Charles H. Hansen, Corp.
11. *Easter Cambiata Hymnal* by Cooper. Published by Hansen, Corp.
12. *Soon Ah Will Be Done* arr. by Clark; No. 5148. Kjos Music Co.
13. *Thanks Be to Thee*, Handel, No. 5103. Kjos Music Co.
14. *My God and I* by Sergei, No. 216. The Kama Co.
15. *This Is My Father's World* by Ringwald. Published by Shawnee Press.

16. *Let Us Break Bread Together* by Currie, No. 1589. C. C. Birchard Co.
17. *Were You There?* by Wilson, No. T2. Bourne Music Co.
18. *God Is My Shepherd* by Clokey, No. 949. C. C. Birchard Co.
19. *O God of Youth* by Darst, No. CM2147. H. W. Gray Co.
20. *Lord, We Cry to Thee* by Dickinson, No. SC212. H. W. Gray Co.

ASSIGNMENTS

1. Why is it so important that teen-agers be involved in the music program in their local church?
2. Discuss what you consider to be the most important qualifications for any Christian leader working with teen-agers.
3. From your own experience, discuss the physical, emotional, spiritual and musical problems characteristic of the adolescent age.
4. Discuss ways of maintaining interest in each rehearsal. Discuss ways in which interest and enthusiasm can be maintained for the choir program throughout the entire year.
5. Plan a complete 45-50 minute rehearsal, showing the numbers to be rehearsed, the various activities to be included, etc.

ADDITIONAL READING

1. *A Guide for Youth Choirs* by Ingram. Published by Abingdon Press.
2. *Music Education for Teen-Agers* by Sur and Schuller. Published by Harper and Bros.
3. *Music Levels in Christian Education* by Tovey. Published by Van Kampen Press.
4. *Raise a Jubilee: Music in Youth Ministry* by Jensen. Published by Methodist Publishing House.
5. *The Boy's Changing Voice* by Mellalieu. Published by Oxford University Press.
6. *Youth Choirs* by Miller. Published by Flammer Company.

6 | SENIOR CHOIRS

After the music director has made the congregation aware of the possibilities of the music ministry and has laid the proper foundations at the earlier age levels, the matter of organizing an effective Senior Choir should be a natural development. The goal of all church singers should be eventual membership in the Senior Choir. This group should epitomize the efforts of the entire music program. These members should be the most spiritual, loyal and thoroughly trained of all of the church's singers.

There are, however, specific problems that confront directors of church senior choirs. These problems can be categorized under two broad headings — problems of administration and problems involved in developing group musicianship. Both of these topics as well as the choice and use of appropriate materials will be considered in this chapter.

ADMINISTRATION

A. *Recruiting and Selecting New Members.* Church senior choir memberships generally begin with the high school graduates or possibly with high school seniors. Socially it would be more ideal if the church were large enough to have a separate college age group, but again this will depend upon local church circumstances. Whether a choir admits members during their late teens or at post-college age makes little difference so far as the basic matters of musicianship and spiritual emphasis are concerned. Imperative, however, is the fact that every Senior Choir member must be a professing Christian — a worthy representative of the Gospel. There is also the matter of whether or not a choir member should be a church member. Again this will vary from one church to another, and the director must recruit his members in accordance with the existing church policy on this matter.

Although pulpit and bulletin announcements are important, nothing replaces personal contact in recruiting new members for the choir. The director must try to instill this ideal in all of his members and especially in the choir's officers. Even so, final arguments such as "not having enough time" must be subdued by the director himself. An ideal Senior Choir membership should be approximately ten percent of the active church membership. To achieve this goal, the director should meet at the beginning of each new season with his music committee, pastor and choir officers to make a list of available and prospective members. After this list is agreed upon by all concerned, a letter of invitation should then be sent out with a return card to be filled out by the prospective member stating his intentions regarding choir membership. This same procedure is then repeated each year, thus assuring the director that he has not overlooked any new talent in the church and that spiritual and musical or social undesirables are not included in the membership. Many directors then require a personal interview or a group conference with all potential members before the first rehearsal.

Other methods for recruiting a new supply of choir members include having a definite recruitment drive, possibly for two weeks, once or several times throughout the year when everyone in the church is aware of this emphasis. It should be cautioned, however, that a certain prestige must always be maintained for the choir. Never should a person be begged to become a choir member. Rather, it should be thought of as a privilege to serve God in this special capacity. Also, survey cards can be passed out periodically throughout the entire congregation to determine musical interest and potential. Further, mention should be made about the problem of getting enough male singers for the choir. Frequently, most choirs have difficulty in securing a sufficient number of men. A director should do all possible to cooperate with the various men's groups in the church — men's Bible classes, brotherhoods, etc., in order to interest as many men as possible in the choir program.

B. *Development of Spiritual Attitudes.* After the director has assembled his new group each year, generally shortly after Labor Day, he then faces the task of molding old and new members into a spiritually effective musical organization. Members must be taught and impressed with the importance of their ministry. Each member must be made to realize that he has a vital place in one of the great heritages of the Christian church. It should be pointed out to him that from the time of Hebrew worship and throughout church history, choirs have been one of the important factors in group worship and in the proclamation of the gospel message. He should be taught to realize that the main purpose of a choir is not mere entertainment or the display of individual talent. Rather, it is the blending of many talents and personalities into a composite force that has unusual possibilities for providing spiritual inspiration, warmth and unity to a service. Each member should be made to realize that during a service his decorum should serve as an example to the congregation as a leader for attitudes of reverence and worship; a leader of enthusiastic congregational singing; a leader with regard to general alertness, attentiveness and respect to the pastor and his message. In general, each member must be made keenly sensitive of his privileged ministry — that of a leader in the worship and praise of Almighty God, and he should seek to use his musical ability to accomplish the spiritual aims and purposes of his church.

Since the spiritual effectiveness of any church choir is directly proportionate to its loyalty and morale, a director must work constantly against the factors that can undermine this. Some of these are:

1. Erratic attendance at rehearsals.
2. Habitual tardiness at rehearsals.
3. Missing the service after attending the rehearsal.
4. Singing in the service without attending the rehearsals.
5. Unrelated foolishness and lack of attention during the rehearsals.
6. Unfriendly attitudes toward other members or the formation of little cliques within the choir.
7. Ill feelings that are voiced publicly rather than privately to the director, such as immediate dislikes to new music, new ideas or suggestions, etc.
8. Members who are concerned about displaying their individual talent or satisfying personal interests rather than working for the good of the entire group.
9. Voicing opinions to others regarding one's disrespect for the director or the organization, especially to those outside of the organization.
10. In general, any action or attitude that dampens the enthusiasm of present or future choir members.

C. *Developing and Maintaining Group Morale and Interest.* Although the chief means of maintaining group interest throughout the year is the music a choir sings — music that consistently inspires, challenges and interests each member — there are other specific factors that also play an important role in this respect. Even though a director should purposely try to maintain a relaxed, friendly relationship with his choir, yet each member must be able to sense a spirit of seriousness and businesslike attitude on the part of the director. This attitude should be evident in the way a director begins and ends rehearsals on time; the way he makes the most effective use of rehearsal time; his supervision of proper records, seating arrangements, robe distribution, follow-ups of delinquent members; distribution, collection and care of music, etc. Not only must a choir member experience spiritual, musical and social satisfaction from the choir, but he must take pride in the fact that he is a member of one of the most vital, progressive and interesting groups in the entire church.

Every church choir should have its own spirit of Christian fellowship. The choir social chairman is especially important in this area of activity. In addition to planned social functions such as parties, after rehearsal refreshments, banquets, etc., the social chairman should lead in welcoming new members and visitors to the choir. This can be done by having periodic socials or receptions for new members. The matter of sending birthday cards, get-well cards, we-miss-you cards, sympathy cards, flowers, etc., to choir members is also a most important item. Other activities that can do much to promote choir interest include: a choir dedication or recognition service at the beginning or close of a season, monthly news letters, weekend retreats, summer camp programs, an annual church music instruction week, an occasional list of new choir members in the bulletin, exchange programs with other church choirs, participation in church choral festivals, and the preparation of special cantatas or programs.

D. *Organization.* Every adult choir needs to adopt a plan of organization. The constitution and by-laws of the group should be clearly stated and easily accessible, especially to the new members. The various details involved in successfully administering a church choir are far too complex for any director, requiring, therefore, a democratic form of organization. This organization can be as simple or as elaborate as is desired. Generally, however, most senior choirs will need at least the following officers: president, vice-president, secretary, treasurer, librarian, social chairman, and robe chairman. The president coordinates the various activities and acts as group administrator. The vice-president takes over in the absence of the president and is usually directly responsible for the promotion and enlistment of new members and the encouragement of absentees to attend rehearsals and services. The secretary is all-important in that she keeps the attendance records and informs the director and officers of the faithfulness of each member. The treasurer is responsible for all finances. In some choirs this is on a small dues basis for each rehearsal while in other organizations a collection plate is passed periodically to meet the various expenses of the group. Often a choir will undertake a special financial project for the church and will attempt to raise funds through special programs and other means. The librarian should see that the music to be used gets into the hands of choir members quickly, is properly returned to the files after its use, and checked out to members who desire to borrow a copy. The librarian should also see that all of the music is stamped, catalogued and filed according to a definite system. It should be the additional responsibility of the librarian to see that all numbers have a minimum reserve supply and that all music is in a state of good repair at all times. The social chairman, as previously stated, should be responsible for all details involved in the group's social functions, sick details, etc. Larger choirs should have section chairmen to aid in the matters of faithfulness. Robe chairmen, usually one for the ladies and one for the men, are very important. These leaders are responsible for having the robes cleaned and repaired as needed. Robe chairmen also keep robe assignment records and assign robes to the new members and visiting soloists. Some choirs have a program chairman, who assumes responsibility for the composition, printing, and distribution of choir programs on special occasions. Often choirs have a publicity chairman to handle all details regarding advertising and promotion of the choir's activities. There may also be a historian appointed to keep a permanent file or scrapbook of programs, clippings, and other interesting memoranda.

E. *Church Library Maintenance.* One of the all-important financial investments in the church is the music library. When one considers the individual cost of each number, plus the hours spent by a director in choosing new music, one soon realizes the importance of maintaining an efficient library. Since most church budgets are rather limited for musical expenditures, it means that all new music must be wisely purchased and the old music ought to be kept in good repair, so that it can be repeated periodically. Occasionally it is wise to spend part of a choir rehearsal in letting all of the members repair the old music. Not only does this get the music in shape, but it also impresses upon the members the need for the proper care of their music.

The two main methods of storing music are keeping it in individual box containers, such as those sold by the Gamble-Hinged Music Company, or keeping the music in individual folders, preferably the three-enclosed-side folders sold by the Educational Music Bureau, No. 120. These may then be filed alphabetically or in individual file drawers according to voice arrangements — SSA,

SATB, SA, SAB, TTBB, etc. With whatever method used, music must be kept dust free and in a dry storage space.

With either of these methods it is wise for the director to keep a card file system so that he can get at a glance the information he desires about each number. This information should include such items as title, composer, arranger or editor, occasion for which useful, whether or not a cappella, difficulty, voice ranges, tessitura problems, and a brief word about that number that will help to give it recall at some future date.

It is also good for the director to keep his personal file of individual copies of music. This is invaluable to a director, although it soon becomes cumbersome for finding music quickly. As with the church card file, it is wise for the director to keep a card file on his own personal music. The information desired should be similar to that mentioned above. Although this filing work may seem at times to be tedious, in the long run it saves many hours for a director when he urgently needs a particular number for a special occasion.

F. *Rehearsal Techniques.* Another of the important areas of choir work to which a director must give careful attention is that of making as much of his limited rehearsal time as possible. Since most church choir rehearsals range from only one to two hours in length each week, one can readily see that if a director has one or two special numbers to prepare, responses to learn and perfect for each service, as well as special programs or cantatas to give several times throughout the year, he must make effective use of every available minute. Although some numbers require more time than others, most directors generally like to have at least four to six weeks for each new number. This means that each rehearsal should include numbers in three stages of development: the introductory stage, the learning stage and the perfecting stage.

The matter of introducing or, better yet, selling new music to a choir is always an interesting challenge to any director. With many people, the old songs are always the best songs, and often there is a great deal of inertia that must be overcome with any worth-while new song. Is there a director who has never experienced the let-down that follows when after singing through a fine new song for the first time, some dear member caustically remarks, "Oh, I don't like that"? This attitude on the part of even one person can often become contagious with the entire group.

Directors have various ways of introducing new music to a choir. One of the newer methods is that of using a professional recording when this is possible. It should be cautioned, however, that never should a choir strive to be mere imitators of the recording. Some directors like to talk about the number and point out in advance some of the musical and textual highlights. Again, it should be cautioned with this method that it is possible for a director to talk so much that the choir members soon are lost in a maze of details. Many directors prefer to get into the song quickly and merely have the choir listen and follow while the song is played by the accompanist. In the final analysis, whatever is said or done or regardless of what method a director uses to introduce a song, the members must catch something of the same interest and enthusiasm that a director himself has for that number. If a director does not feel that kind of interest for a new number, he has no right to expect his members to respond differently.

After the song has been introduced and sung several times in its entirety so that the members have gained an overall impression of the number, the director must begin a more concentrated effort on the individual problems within the song itself. In this stage of development the song is seldom sung in its entirety; rather, each of the various problems is worked out in slow motion tempo. A director should be able to foresee in advance these troublesome spots in a new number and give these places the most emphasis and drill. Typical problem places where average singers will make mistakes include:

1. Difficult melodic intervals — i.e. jumps of Augmented 2nds, 4ths, etc.
2. Abrupt changes in melodic and rhythmic patterns.
3. Altered chords and chords of 7ths and 9ths.
4. Chromatic melodic passages.
5. Changes in mode — major to minor, etc.
6. Changes in key or modulations.
7. High tessituras.

The third and last stage of development is the perfecting stage. Generally such work is done on the songs that will be used on the following Sunday. After the number has been introduced and sung in its entirety, after the various details such as right notes, rhythms, entrances, intonation problems, etc., have been carefully worked out, there comes the final stage of putting everything together as it actually should be performed. Here must be re-emphasized the emotional understanding of the text, the interpretative possibilities of the song — phrasings, inflections, nuances, diction, etc.

For every rehearsal a director must keep in mind that a change of pace is mandatory. Voices must be eased; minds, nerves, emotions relaxed. This can be done by changes of activity, by contrasts in styles and moods of songs sung, by time-outs for discussing future plans and organizational business, as well as time-outs for just plain fun and fellowship.

Many of the mere mechanics of a rehearsal often are time consuming. For example, the transition from one number to the next can be a time for dissipating conversation while the slower members find new music. The services of a good librarian are needed in this regard to insure that all music is passed out or in the folders before the rehearsal begins. It is also helpful if the director writes on a blackboard the order of the numbers to be rehearsed. It is important that the accompanist can play all new music accurately and confidently. This means that a director should make every effort to give the accompanist new music at least one week in advance of the actual rehearsal. This not only saves time for the entire group but also spares the accompanist much personal embarrassment.

For a rehearsal, most directors prefer the use of a piano rather than the organ because of the piano's greater percussiveness. It is also felt that it is better to practice in a smaller room than in the church chancel, especially where the seats can be arranged in such a way that the individual parts can hear each other more readily. Occasionally it is wise for a director to use a tape recorder during a rehearsal so that choir members can hear for themselves such items as diction, blend, tone quality, attacks and releases. Directors often disagree on the matter of the place and importance of formal vocal drills and exercises in rehearsals. This entire problem of group drill will to a large extent be governed by the seriousness of the group itself. For an amateurish group, formal drill should be kept to a minimum. However, for a group more desirous of improvement, much more time can be spent in gaining finer tone quality, precision and control. Many directors like to use the Sunday hymns, responses, or familiar songs as a way of "warming up" the voices and for emphasizing the basic vocal concepts such as vowel consciousness, open throats and body support. Further, formal drill and the teaching of vocal concepts need not be limited to the early part of the rehearsal. A director should be able to improvise easy exercises to correct particular problems whenever the need arises within a song itself.

There is also the matter of the actual order or arrangement of a rehearsal, especially with regard to utilizing the singers when their voices are at their best and their minds the most alert. Some directors like to work on new numbers during the early part of a rehearsal; others like to use this time for perfecting numbers; still others feel that this is the ideal time for working out particular problems. With experience, however, a director should be able to realize when a group is the most productive and concentrate during that time on whatever needs the greatest emphasis. With any plan, though, a director should never allow his rehearsals to become stereotyped.

A sample rehearsal could be planned as follows:

1. A brief devotional time — Scripture reading, prayer, generally by the choir's president.

8-10 minutes:

2. A time of warm-up — vocal drills, work on the hymns, responses, familiar songs, etc. An emphasis on vocal concepts, blend, sensitive listening. An instruction in some phase of basic harmony.

12-15 minutes:

3. Sing through and perfect this Sunday's numbers for final performance.

10-15 minutes:

4. Introduce and read through several new numbers for future use, although some of these numbers might be thought of as merely sight singing practice.

12-15 minutes:

5. Intensive practice on just the spots that have various musical problems from the music that was introduced in previous weeks.

5-10 minutes:

6. Break — announcements, discussion of future plans, organizational details, etc.

10-15 minutes:

7. Sing through Sunday's numbers again from the choir loft. This provides the director with a good opportunity to listen to the choir from various parts of the auditorium in order to check the balance between the choir and accompanist, etc.

8. Closing devotions followed by periodic social times.

Several miscellaneous suggestions regarding rehearsals are listed briefly as follows:

1. Thoroughly "think through" and plan each rehearsal in advance. Keep things moving and interesting during the rehearsal. However, members must have a sense of accomplishment when finished. Keep a record of all rehearsals. After each rehearsal analyze and evaluate the effectiveness of the rehearsal.

2. Always have more to do than it seems it is possible to accomplish. A major project is always stimulating — cantatas, special programs, preparing a record, etc.
3. Be able to have fun with the choir. However, don't strive to be a "funny person." Let the humor be spontaneous. Be patient with mistakes. It is always better to make a joke of the mistake rather than to scold, become sarcastic, or to embarrass anyone. Keep in mind that these singers are amateurs — singing primarily because they wish to serve God and to enjoy the pleasure of singing. Don't destroy these desires!
4. Be generous with the compliments, yet at the same time keep higher goals for the choir to attain.
5. Be considerate and thoughtful of the accompanist. Acknowledge her contribution often before the entire group as well as privately.
6. Be sure that your rehearsal room is well ventilated and well lighted.
7. Be conscious of sparing the voices whenever possible. For example, high passages for tenors and sopranos can often be worked out in drill an octave lower, etc.
8. Practice in such a way that the inner parts are close to each other and the outer parts close to each other as well.
9. When practicing larger works such as cantatas it is wise to do some of your practicing from the last number to the first rather than always starting from the beginning. This insures confidence for the ending or the climax of the work rather than having confidence only for a good start.
10. End the rehearsal on a "high note" — have the members go home feeling good.

G. *Matters of Performance.* After the director has prepared the choir musically as thoroughly as possible, there still remain certain details of conduct to be learned by the choir for the actual performance itself. Not only should the various mechanics of performance be taught and discussed in the rehearsal, but a director should strive to have approximately fifteen minutes before the Sunday service to take care of a number of last minute details. After the choir members have been robed and assembled, the director or the choir president should give final instructions regarding seating arrangements, the order of the service, etc. This pre-service assembling should also provide enough time for a sufficient warmup, as well as a brief review of the numbers to be performed.

However, if the numbers are not well enough learned by Sunday, too much intensive practice and cramming will generally tend to make the choir tense for the service. It should also be customary for the pastor, board member, choir president, or director to lead in brief devotions before going into the service.

The goal of all choral performance should always be that of inspiring an audience with some truth of the gospel message. Many church choirs perform with adequate technical facility but leave little spiritual impression upon their listeners. Choirs of this type actually appear apologetic about having an audience listen to their songs. Individual choir members appear visibly surprised when an audience does show a favorable response to a number. Few members show with their faces any of the spirit and mood of the song they are singing. Even the spontaneity and aggressiveness that was theirs at the rehearsals is now completely lacking. Somehow and in some way each director must find a way of instilling individual leadership in each member. The choir must be constantly challenged with an intense desire to communicate the message of each song to every listener.

Other basic concepts regarding performance that a director must try to impress upon each member are listed briefly as follows:

1. Keep your attention concentrated on the director at all times. Don't let your eyes wander around the audience. Don't get into the habit of simply staring into the music when it really isn't necessary.

2. Hold your music at eye level so that you may easily observe and reflect the director's facial and hand movements.

3. Be continually thinking ahead so that attacks, releases, special effects and climaxes do not catch you unaware.

4. Maintain your poise and keep going no matter what happens. Forget past mistakes. Make up in the new phrase what you have missed in the previous phrase. Remember, even though you have made a mistake or you hear the mistakes of others, the general effect may still be pleasing and the mistake unnoticed by the average listener.

5. Be natural and friendly with the audience, yet keep a poise and dignity in such matters as rising, sitting, conspicuous clothing or accessories, personal conversations, undue coughing or clearing of throats especially before or after a number, or any action that might attract attention to you rather than to your ministry.

6. Stay within the character of the song even when not singing — during the introduction, interludes, postludes, rests,

solo parts, etc. During these times center your attention on the director, not on your music or on the audience. Breathe deeply during these times, look relaxed and poised, and be anticipating the next entrance.

7. Guard your voice carefully. Do all that is possible to keep it in the best condition at all times. Refrain from excessive yelling or straining, drafts, undue physical fatigue, or heavy eating just before singing.

II. GROUP MUSICIANSHIP

In addition to the above mentioned administrative problems that confront church choir directors, there remain the more technical musical problems that must be dealt with in developing group musicianship. These include the following: Lack of sight reading ability; lack of confident singing; poor intonation; poor blend; poor diction; lack of proper balance; ineffective interpretation.

It is good for a director to know in advance something about these musical problems that he is certain to find with any amateur group, and to have definite procedures in mind for lessening and resolving such problems. There are, however, certain general principles to follow for working out any of these musical problems.

One of the first of these principles is that of simplifying the problem to its lowest common denominator. For example, if the problem for a certain passage is a rhythmic one, the director should find ways of working on this problem without employing other factors such as words or pitches. Another important principle is that of repetition — making sure that the new habit or pattern is sufficiently impressed upon the mind to insure its permanency. It should be mentioned, though, that each repetition is always done with a purpose. The choir should always be aware of why they are repeating each time they are asked to do so. It should also be mentioned that in the initial stages of working out a problem, all such drill should be done in slow motion tempo with each repetition gradually getting the problem developed to its normal tempo.

A third principle that a director should keep in mind when working out various musical problems with a choir is that of giving variety to all drill. This may be achieved by varying the tempo, the dynamics, or by varying the group working on the problem. For example, if the men have been working on a rhythmic problem, let the women try that same problem while the men listen, etc. Perhaps for the next repetition the words could be used rather than just a neutral syllable, with finally all the voice parts being added. To keep the whole choir studying and to provide harmonic background, it often is good to allow one or two parts to drill while the other parts hum. No matter what method a director uses to gain variety in his drill work, he must constantly guard against disinterest and mental fatigue. Continuous repetition without any variety will soon result in boredom, which in turn leads to a point of diminishing returns for further development.

A. *Lack of Sight Reading Ability.* A musical problem common to most volunteer choirs is the lack of individuals who can read music with adequate facility. However, this musical deficiency should never create a hopeless situation. Choral music can be taught and learned by mere imitation and rote if the director will use suitable songs and approach the group in a helpful, patient manner. Further, directors must have confidence in the fact that individuals will acquire adequate skill naturally as they gain musical experience; and more formal sight singing techniques can be taught the average singer by a qualified director.

There are several basic concepts regarding sight reading that a director should try to develop with his singers. Of utmost importance is the fact that amateur singers need confidence. They need to be encouraged and made to realize that the ability to read music is natural and normal for anyone. It is not some mysterious talent, nor is it totally dependent upon a great deal of technical musical knowledge. Directors must also develop the proper attitude for trying new music. Singers should be encouraged to attempt new music with wholeheartedness and confidence even at the expense of gross error. Members should also be encouraged to take advantage of every opportunity to practice and improve their music reading ability. For example, this can be done during congregational singing or while other parts are rehearsing. Singers should also be constantly challenged to force their eyes to read ahead, to see groups of notes as well as only the direction of individual tones. However, in the initial stages of a group's development, it is far more important that a director stimulate musical interest and desire with the group rather than merely teach formal musical information or conduct repetitive drills. In the final analysis, the best way to begin to sight-read music is simply to be exposed to a great deal of singing.

As a choir develops in its interest, desire and musical experience, a director should begin to teach his singers a more definite technique for reading music. This involves instruction in rhythm and intervals. The technical problem of sight reading is that of learning to coordinate a physical sensation of the rhythmic pulsations and patterns with the eye and ear recognition of the distance (intervals) between tones, so that any new music can be sung quickly and confidently.

The problem of rhythm is not merely having an intellectual understanding of the arithmetical divisions of a measure, although this knowledge is helpful and eventually needful. Foremost, rhythm must be felt physically. This means that each choir member must sense a firm, underlying beat or pulsation to the music. This assumes, then, that a director is capable of maintaining and conducting a steady beat to any song. It is well said that no conductor should attempt any interpretative conducting until he has first learned to maintain a steady rhythmic type of leadership. Directors use various methods for teaching this concept. Some choir leaders like to have each singer tap his foot during the early stages of learning a song. Often directors teach rhythm by having the choir clap the rhythmic patterns while beating the main pulsations with their feet. Other conductors have the choir chant the rhythm patterns, using a neutral sound such as "la," "ta," etc.

The teaching of intervals (the exact measurement of distance between any two tones) is part of the total instruction in a basic study of harmony that a director should try to teach his choir once their experience and interest warrant it. In addition to the study of intervals, this basic instruction in harmony should also include a study of chord construction. This involves such knowledge as: All chords are built on the interval of thirds (either major or minor thirds); every chord contains a root, third and fifth; an understanding of such terms as tonic, sub-dominant, dominant, chords with added sevenths, etc. Members should also be made conscious of the note of a chord that their part is singing, especially of thirds, sevenths, and dissonant notes. This is especially needful for the sake of good intonation at cadences. It is also helpful in the matter of finding one's starting note for a song if members are taught to listen to the tonic note after the introduction and made to realize that their part will invariably be either this tonic note or a third of fifth above or below this tone.

The following is a suggested procedure for teaching a formal sight singing technique:

1. First Stage. Learn songs mainly by imitation and rote — going over the song enough times, practicing individual parts, etc., until the song is learned. Singers are made aware only of the general melodic directions of the music. During this time, the main concern of the director should be to develop interest and confidence in his singers, to create a desire for the singers to improve their individual abilities,

and to provide an adequate musical experience for future development. Rhythmically, a director's main emphasis should be that of getting the singers to feel the basic beat in music.

2. Second Stage. After a proper amount of time in the first stage (this will vary greatly from one group to another), begin teaching the following:

   a. Notation — an understanding of the keyboard and its relationship to the staffs and the letter names of notes. Rhythm — the meaning of time signatures, arithmetical values of notes, etc.

   b. A concept of half and whole steps. This can be done by first showing the choir the organization of the keyboard. Then, by ear, the singers should develop the ability to move their voices in either direction by these half and whole step movements.

   c. A concept of scale building. All major scales are built by half and whole steps. The half steps are between the third and fourth degrees as well as between the seventh and eighth steps of the scale.

   d. A concept of singing intervals. The ability to sing from the tonic or first note of a scale to any other degree of the scale. (Keep in mind that the ear must always be trained before the eye.) It is often helpful to use and associate familiar songs that begin with these intervals that singers can remember and use to find the desired interval.

   e. A concept of the various names of intervals — Perfects, Majors, Minors, Diminished, Augmented.

   f. A concept of recognizing the exact interval between any two tones. Think of the bottom note as the beginning note of a scale. If the top note is in the scale of that note it is either a Perfect or Major Interval, the Perfect Intervals being the eighths, fifths, and fourths. Seconds, Thirds, Sixths, and Sevenths, then, are Major Intervals. If the top note is a half step lower than it would be in a Major Interval, it is a Minor Interval. If the top note is a half step lower than it would be in a Perfect Interval, it is a Diminished Interval. A Diminished Interval can also be a Minor Interval that is further lowered by a half step. When either a Major or Perfect Interval is raised by a half step, it is known as an Augmented Interval.

g. A concept of measuring and singing intervals downward as well as up.

h. A concept of chord construction:

   (1) A three tone chord known as a triad is the basic chord of all harmony.

   (2) All triads consist of a:

   (3) All triads as well as larger chords (4-5 tone chords) are built on the interval of a third.

   (4) Triads are given a Roman Numeral according to the degree of the scale upon which they are built.

An Example of the Various Chords in the Key of F

   (a) Other names by which these chords are known: I or Tonic Chord; II or Super Tonic Chord; III or Mediant Chord; IV or Sub-Dominant Chord; V or Dominant Chord; VI or Sub-Mediant Chord; VII or Leading Tone Chord.

   (b) The most commonly used chords in music are the tonic, sub-dominant and dominant.

   (c) When an additional interval of a third is added to a basic triad, it is known as a chord with a 7th. For example, in the key of F, a V Chord with the added 7th would. be called a V7 Chord or a Dominant 7th Chord, and would consist of the notes, CEGB♭. When another interval of a third is added to a chord with a 7th, it would be called a chord with a 9th, etc.

   (5) Chords are often designated simply by their individual sound. Example, the above I Chord in the Key of F could simply be called an "F Major Chord"; the above II Chord in the Key of F could simply be called a "G Minor Chord"; the III Chord an "A Minor Chord"; the IV Chord a "B♭ Major Chord"; the V Chord a "C Major Chord"; or with the added 7th, a "C7th Chord"; the VI Chord a "D Minor Chord"; the VII Chord an "E Diminished Chord."

(6) In learning to recognize chord construction, think of the notes as though they were arranged in triad position (built on intervals of thirds). Then try to realize the note of the triad (root, third, fifth, seventh, etc.) as it applies to each part.

Example of a Chord Progression for the Key of F

I   I (inv)   V7   I

(a) In the first I Chord (FAC), the fifth of the chord is in the soprano and alto parts, the third of the chord is in the tenor part, and the root of the chord is in the bass voice.

(b) In the second chord, which is an inversion of a I Chord (FAC), the third of the chord is in the soprano, the root of the chord is in the alto, while the fifth of the chord is in the tenor and bass parts, at the interval of an octave apart.

(c) In the V7 Chord, (CEGBb), the fifth of the chord is in the soprano, the third of the chord is in the alto, the seventh of the chord is in the tenor, and the root of the chord is in the bass.

(d) In the last I Chord, the root of the chord is in the soprano, the fifth of the chord is in the alto, the third of the chord is in the tenor, and the root of the chord is in the bass.

(e) If the above chord progression had been played on the piano or organ as an introduction for a song, after the playing of the last chord, the tonic note F would be the one tone that would be predominantly heard. Upon the establishment of this tone, each member should immediately mentally sing to himself the FAC Chord. Then, to find one's pitch for the first chord of this progression, the sopranos and altos would simply find the fifth of the chord below the tonic; the tenors would sing up a third from the tonic, while the basses would retain the tonic note. The next problem would be that of trying to retain the tonic sound throughout the entire song or until a new key is established, since all of the notes within a song are closely related to the tonic note.

Example of How to Find One's Starting Note for the Above Chord Progression

I use the following syllabus in mimeographed form each year with my senior church choirs. Ideally, there should be a special week of church music emphasis each year when various subjects such as sight singing, song leading, tone quality, and hymnology would be taught all choir members and others especially interested. However, if this does not seem possible, it is still most gratifying to see the great improvement that can be made with a choir even in one year's time simply by spending a few minutes consistently in each rehearsal on some phase of this subject.

SUGGESTIONS FOR IMPROVING ONE'S SIGHT READING ABILITY

I. An understanding of the keyboard.

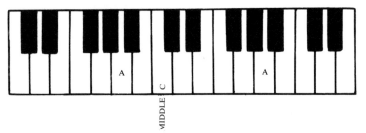

A. Uses the first seven letters of the alphabet (A through G).
B. The note "A" is always the white note between the 2nd and 3rd black notes in each group of three black notes.
C. Composed of half and whole steps:
   1. A half step is from a white note to a black note or vice versa, or from a white note to another white note when there is no black note between the white notes. — Example, between the "b's" and "c's" and between the "e's" and "f's."
   2. A whole step is composed of two half steps.
      a. Be able to sing a half step up or down from any tone.
      b. Be able to sing a whole step up or down from any tone.

II. An understanding of the relationship of the keyboard to the staffs.

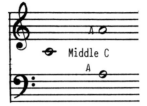

III. An understanding of the construction of Major Scales.

An Example of a Major Scale

A. This is the scale for the key of F since the beginning note of the scale (the tonic note) is the note "F." Hence, the key of F will always have one flat (b) in the key signature, which will always be on the note "B."

B. Every Major Scale is composed of eight notes, with the first and eighth notes being the same tone only an octave apart.

C. Every Major Scale is composed of whole steps between each note except between the third and fourth notes and between the seventh and eighth notes, which will always have half steps.

D. Every scale must move diatonically. That is:
   1. Must make some use of every successive letter. Example – in the scale of F one cannot move from an "A" to an "A♯," but rather it must be notated as an "A" to a "Bb," etc.
   2. Can make only one use of each successive letter of the scale.

E. Miscellaneous:
   1. A Sharp (♯) raises a note a half step. A double sharp (x) raises a note a whole step.
   2. A Flat (b) lowers a note a half step. A double flat (bb) lowers a note a whole step.
   3. A Natural (♮) destroys the effect of either a flat or sharp.

IV. Intervals – the distance between any two notes.
   A. A note that would move from F^1 to F^8 would be an interval of an eighth or an octave.
   B. A note that would move from F to E would be an interval of a seventh. F to D would be an interval of a sixth; F to C a fifth; F to Bb a fourth; F to A a third; F to G a second.
   C. Intervals of 8ths, 5ths and 4ths are technically known as *Perfect Intervals.*
   D. Any interval other than a Perfect Interval where the top note is still in the scale of the bottom note is technically known as a *Major Interval.*
   E. When the top note is a half step lower than what the Major Interval would be it is known as a *Minor Interval.*
   F. When the top note is a half step lower than what the Perfect Interval

would be it is known as a *Diminished Interval*. A Diminished Interval can also be when the top note is a half step lower than a Minor Interval.

G. When the top note of either a Major or Perfect Interval is raised by a half step it is known as an *Augmented Interval*.

H. Helps for hearing and singing these intervals:

    1. Major 2nds — just up a whole step.

    2. Major 3rds — "My Jesus I Love Thee."

    3. Perfect 4ths — "Stand Up for Jesus."

    4. Perfect 5ths — the top note of the Tonic Chord — "There Is a Fountain."

    5. Major 6ths — "My Bonnie Lies Over the Ocean."

    6. Major 7ths — half step below the octave.

    7. Perfect 8ths — octave.

I. Helps for recognizing intervals. Write out and study the following scales. One must be able to think and visualize any scale in his mind:

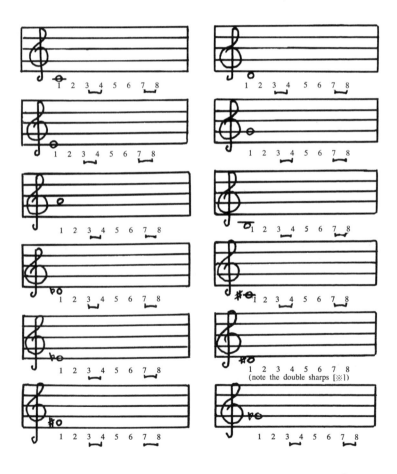

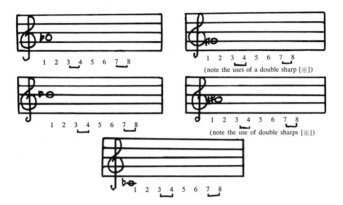

J. Identify and sing each of these intervals:

1. A Major 3rd up from C_____
2. A Minor 3rd up from C_____
3. A Perfect 4th up from D_____
4. A Major 6th up from E_____
5. A Minor 6th up from G_____
6. A Major 7th up from B_____
7. A Minor 7th up from B♭_____
8. A Perfect 5th up from A_____
9. A Minor 2nd up from F♯_____
10. An Aug. 4th up from A♭_____
11. An Aug. 5th up from D♭_____
12. A Minor 7th up from G♯_____
13. An Aug. 4th up from F_____
14. A Dim. 5th up from C_____
15. A Dim. 4th up from F_____
16. An Aug. 6th up from E_____
17. A Dim. 3rd up from F_____
18. An Aug. 4th up from C♯_____
19. A Dim. 7th up from C_____
20. An Aug. 3rd up from E_____

K. The *Tonic Chord* for any key consists of the 1st, 3rd, and 5th notes of a scale.

Example of the Tonic Chord for Key of F

L. Helps for hearing and singing intervals downward:
1. A Minor 2nd down — just a half step down.
2. A Major 2nd down — just a whole step down.
3. A Minor 3rd down — the second tone of "The Star Spangled Banner."

    4. A Major 3rd down — "Cleanse Me, O God."
    5. A Perfect 4th down — The 5th of the Tonic Chord only an octave lower.
    6. A Perfect 5th down—the third tone of "The Star Spangled Banner."
    7. A Minor 6th down — the 3rd of the Tonic Chord only an octave lower.
    8. A Major 6th down — "Nobody Knows the Trouble I've Seen."
    9. A Minor 7th down — "On a Rugged Hill."
  10. A Major 7th down — a half step from the octave.
  11. A Perfect 8th down — octave.

V. A Word of Encouragement. Even though all of this seems involved and complicated to you now, you will be surprised how with a little study and practice all of this can be readily learned so that your ear and eye become correlated to make all of this practical for improving your sight reading ability.

B. *Lack of Confident Singing.* Another musical problem with which a director must deal is lack of confidence. A non-confident choir can be easily detected by even the most casual listener. It is reflected in the members' stoic faces, in their listless bodily attitudes, by their lack of contact with the audience, and by their general appearance of timidity. Musically, a non-confident choir will be characterized by the following:

    1. Sluggish tempos.
    2. Hesitant attacks and releases.
    3. Poor diction.
    4. Scooping and slurring up and down to tones.
    5. Thin tone quality.
    6. Lack of contrasts in interpretation — singing everything at the same dynamic level.
    7. Lack of attention to the director.

One of the chief tasks for any director to overcome is self-consciousness in the average singer. There are several basic fears that most beginning singers have. They are:

    1. The fear of the sound of their own voice.
    2. The fear of the congregation.
    3. The fear of singing wrong notes.
    4. The fear of singing wrong words.
    5. The fear of not being accepted by the other more experienced members.
    6. The fear of not singing in tune.
    7. The fear of singing when they are not supposed to sing.

With volunteer choirs a director's attitude should always be that wrong notes are never as important as the overall performance, nor is a mistake as important as the self-confidence of the members of the choir. Directors should avoid any gestures that might add to the singer's fears — scowls of displeasure, flatting or sharping indications, etc.

There are several fundamental concepts that a director must teach his choir regarding looking and sounding more confident. For example, singers should be taught the importance of good posture not only for better tone production but also for good appearance as well. They should be taught to stand with the weight of the body on the forward part of the feet, with the arms slightly out from the body thus reflecting the buoyancy of their posture. They should also be taught to hold their music with uniformity at eye level so that they may easily observe and reflect the director's facial and hand movements. The ability to project sincerely the spirit and mood of a song with the eyes and facial expressions can come, however, only as members are completely aware of and impressed with the meaning and mood of a song. In the final analysis, then, it can be said that basically a choir's personality is merely a reflection of its director's personality and leadership.

Choir members must constantly be challenged regarding aggressiveness in their attacks. There often is the tendency to wait for someone else to begin, with the result that many church choirs usually get started with a full tone on about the third beat of each phrase. There are several possible explanations for such poor attacks. It may be that the director is not giving a sufficiently clear preparatory or breathing motion. It may be that the director has not commanded the complete eye attention of the group before starting; or the director may never have taught the choir the importance of knowing the first few notes and words of each new phrase sufficiently well so that they don't give in to the natural tendency of looking into their music just as they are about to sing.

Directors should teach their members that good attacks are basically the result of proper physical and mental preparation just prior to the actual singing. This, then, involves the following:

1. Hearing the pitch mentally.
2. Preparing one's bodily support.
3. Preparing one's jaw and tongue positions for the vowel sound to follow.

If this preparation begins after the tone begins, poor attacks are inevitable. Technically speaking, good attacks are the result of what many vocal teachers call the "shock of the glottis." This merely means that at the moment of the air passing through the larynx to make a sound by means of the vocal cords, these cords are firmly stretched at just the right tension and the note struck is exactly the pitch required without any pitch adjustment being necessary. This then involves the problem of synchronizing two factors — breath and vocal cords.

When releasing a tone, members should be taught that there should be a feeling that the jaw is maintained in a relaxed position throughout the duration of the tone while the necessary tongue action and bodily support coordinate to accomplish the final cut-off. This keeps the throat open and the cut-off free from any harsh "barking" sounds. The higher the pitch of the note to be released, the greater the problem of achieving this type of smooth cut-off, necessitating ever greater use of one's bodily support.

The problem of scooping and slurring from one tone to another usually can be attributed to the following lazy vocal habits: spending too much time on initial and final consonants rather than getting into each new vowel quickly, and not maintaining proper bodily support so that each vowel sound is held with intensity for its complete duration. In addition to making people vowel conscious, one of the best ways of overcoming this problem is to practice singing each note with a slight staccato attack.

Since truly effective interpretation for most amateur singers generally seems overly exaggerted, audiences usually must condition themselves to sluggish, uninspiring choral singing. This problem no doubt accounts for the fact that programs entirely choral are not usually well attended and do not have the inspirational appeal that they should have. Directors, then, must teach their members that effective interpretation can not be based on what may seem right or normal while they are in the process of singing. Effective choral singing must have marked contrasts in tempos and dynamics as well as real rhythmic vitality if it is to have audience appeal. Members must be taught the importance of such concepts that every word within a phrase does not receive equal importance, but rather the unimportant words must give motion and lead to the important words. They must also be taught that even every syllable of a word is not sung with equal importance. This implies a realization that syllables of words are sung in the same proportion of stress that the syllables have when properly spoken and that in vocal music the treatment of words takes precedence over the treatment of the music. For example:

Fá - thĕr;   cŏm - pás - siŏn;   bĕ - giń

All these suggestions can be summarized by saying simply that the mind as well as the voice must remain alert throughout the entire song if the song is to be meaningful and worthy of an audience's attention.

C. *Poor Intonation.* The inability to sing exactly on pitch or in tune is another musical problem common to most singers. The answer to this problem is basically that of developing a proper technique for tone production and that of listening sensitively to each tone sung so that necessary adjustments are made quickly.

Proper vocal technique for tone production, whether for choir or solo singing, is dependent upon three main factors:

1. A relaxed lower jaw, which in turn produces a firm, open throat.
2. A relaxed, arched, forward tongue, which in turn gives high arched resonance and forwardness to a tone.
3. A feeling of good bodily support, which in turn gives steadiness to a tone.

If any of these factors is lacking, intonation problems will result. For example, if the jaw is tight and the throat restricted, this will cause a squeezed, harsh tone which is likely to sound sharp. If the tongue position is poor, the tone will likely sound breathy, throaty and flat. If the bodily support is lacking, the tone is likely to be thin or "white," unsteady, with an over-abundance of vibrato which in turn produces a tremolo or indefinite pitch.

With respect to the importance of bodily support or the use of good breathing habits, singers must be taught and impressed with the fact that this type of breathing is nothing more than the development of their most natural breathing. This can be pointed out by drawing their attention to the deep body breathing of an infant lying on its back. This process of simply relaxing and enlarging the entire intercostal muscle area around the ribs, lower chest and abdomen is often compared by some directors to the playing of an accordion. As the body is filled with new air there must be an expansiveness in the body to make room for that air. As the air is used there will be contraction in that same area. Singers must be taught always to take more breath than is needed each time they breathe, with a feeling that this breath originates in the stomach rather than in the chest. The control and use of that breath is accomplished with a feeling of a steady pull in and up from the upper stomach or the area between the cavity of the chest and the abdomen, technically known as the diaphragm. With volunteer choirs, however, it is better to approach the entire matter of breathing in a natural way rather than in a more formal or abstract manner. More can be accomplished simply by talking in terms of "lift," "pull," "support" than in more technical terms or by the use of various exercises for making the stomach region protrude or the diaphragmatic muscle move quickly. Basically, whether sitting or standing, adequate breathing and support will be achieved by amateur singers simply by having them maintain a buoyant posture and by having them keep a raised chest (yet free of tenseness).

Another basic vocal concept that has a definite effect on intonation is an understanding of the difference between closed and open vowel sounds. The main closed vowels are $\overline{oo}$ and ee. All other vowel sounds are open. Except for soprano voices, all voices in their upper registers should sing with more of the $\overline{oo}$ or ee resonance while in the lower registers there should be more of the Ah and O resonance. The soprano high tones should naturally take on more of the Ah resonance, without, however, sounding harsh or "blatty." In the high register the sopranos should not let the articulation of consonants interfere with this Ah resonance. Tenors often are the cause of much poor intonation when singing high, simply by singing their tones with an open or chest tone quality rather than with a closed or head tone quality.

There are other factors, too, that can contribute to poor intonation. It may be that certain singers are trying for too big a quality, thus losing the control and focus of their tones. Again, this is especially true in the upper registers of voices. Some directors work on this upper register problem merely by having singers imitate their own examples of proper and improper tone quality. Others teach the natural change in vowel color as voices move up and down. For example, in the upper registers, the "A" vowels tend to sound like the "ee's"; the "Ah" sounds more like an "Uh"; the "O" more like the "$\overline{oo}$." Some vocal teachers speak of this upper register quality as the "covered voice," while others approach it by first developing a head-falsetto tone quality and then gradually amalgamating the lower register with this head resonance until a full resonant quality is developed throughout the entire voice.

A director may find it necessary to experiment with the various acoustical properties in a room or auditorium in order to improve a choir's intonation. Such items as draperies, the relationship of the choir to the accompanist, the size of the audience, all have a great deal to do with this problem. Poorly ventilated rooms can also affect intonation. Often poor intonation is caused simply by the lack of mental interest or proper stimulation for a certain number, which will result in flatting, while over-excitement or extreme nervousness may result in sharping.

There are several ways in which a director can encourage keener listening habits and in so doing achieve better intonation from his choir. Basic is the necessity of practicing a great deal unaccompanied. Another good rehearsal technique is that of singing a rather sustained number slowly, holding the chord on each beat until every individual makes the necessary vocal and ear adjustments for exact pitch.

A director should continually be aware of the voice part that has the third of the chord, especially when that chord is the last chord of a phrase. This voice part must be perfectly on pitch; otherwise, the entire chord will be out of tune. Also, it should be noted that the seventh of any chord, because of our system of keyboard tuning, will generally cause intonation problems as well. Many choral directors suggest the following formula based on the "mean tone" system of tuning: "Sharp the third and seventh degrees of the scale as well as to a slight degree the sixth degree of the scale. Flat slightly the fourth degree of the scale." Chromatic passages, too, are difficult for many singers to sing on pitch, as the natural tendency is to move more than a half step at a time. Repeated tones involving vowel changes are also likely to cause intonation problems, especially in the upper ranges. Often a director may find that intonation problems for particular songs can be eliminated simply by raising or lowering the key a half step, or by practicing the song in a slightly higher key than the one in which it will be performed.

D. *Poor Blend.* The problem of blend is closely related to that of intonation, since it too is basically a matter of training the choir in tone consciousness and in attentive listening habits.

Choir members must be impressed with the fact that a good tone has the following characteristics:

1. A quality of roundness, richness and pleasantness rather than one of flatness and harshness.
2. A feeling of flow, flexibility and ease rather than a sense of strain.
3. A steady, unwavering quality rather than one with a "wobble."
4. A forward, projected quality rather than one that is throaty and breathy.
5. A quality of clearness and naturalness rather than one of distortion or affectation.
6. The quality of correct pitch — good intonation.
7. A sensitive, expressive quality — one that reflects the emotional meanings of individual words.

Achieving the fine balance between a spirit of enthusiasm and spontaneity and a controlled group tone is always a challenging problem for any director. Often the axiom is given by directors to their singers that if they hear only their own voice they are singing too loudly. If they can't hear themselves at all, they aren't singing loudly enough.

Although vocal production is basically the same for either solo or choral singing, and though it is generally agreed that proper vibrato and individual distinctiveness can be retained in choral singing, yet it is also true that each choir member must learn to color his voice in such a way that it will blend with the voices he hears around him. This does not mean, however, that a voice should be darkened to the extent that it sounds hooty, hollow, or lifeless. It simply means that good blend is not dependent upon hearing individual voices, beautiful though they may be; rather, it is dependent upon the convergence of all voices into one total group sound.

There are several important factors that specifically contribute to poor blend. These are as follows:

1. Lack of desire to produce a beautiful tone.
2. Problems of intonation as previously discussed.
3. Predominance of individual voices.
4. Faulty diction.
5. Lack of rhythmic precision.
6. Failure to listen to the other voice parts.
7. Uncontrolled vibratos resulting in a tremolo or a "wobble."

A vibrato is natural and normal with correct tone production. A voice freely produced will of necessity have a vibrato of four to six vibrations per second. Faulty vocal production such as lack of breath support, throat restrictions, or throat muscles that do not have enough firmness will result in either a tremolo or a "wobble." A tremolo will have eight or more vibrations per second while the "wobble" will have four or less vibrations per second. To correct these forms of faulty vibrato, work especially on the o͞o and Ah vowels, singing these sounds with as straight a tone quality as possible. This requires a sensation of actually over-breathing or using more breath than is necessary to produce the tone.

There are several techniques that directors use to improve a choir's blend. Unaccompanied singing, of course, is basic. Also, it can be helpful during the rehearsal if the seats are arranged in such a way that members are able to hear other parts as well as just their own. When two voice parts have a close harmonic relationship, it is good to let these parts sing duets in slow motion with each other in order to get more awareness of the other part. The use of a good tape recorder can also be beneficial in this regard. Humming, "o͞oing," singing a song on only one vowel sound at a time, unison singing, and singing in groups of quartets are other methods for developing ensemble and blend consciousness.

E. *Poor Diction.* "I enjoyed the choir but I could hardly understand a word they sang." This typical response is a common experience for most church choir directors, and, unfortunately, it is usually deserved. It is difficult for amateur singers to realize the difficulty listeners have in catching and understanding what is being sung. Choir members must be made to realize that not only is good tone closely related to good diction, but there must be a certain amount of exaggeration in choral diction, more than that used in normal conversation, if the words of a song are to be understood.

Basically, the problem of good diction can be generalized for volunteer singers with two fundamental concepts: (1) a complete textual, emotional and musical understanding of the song with an intense desire to communicate that message to the listeners; (2) achieving rhythmic precision of the words.

In a more technical sense, choirs with more musical maturity should be taught that good diction is dependent upon: (1) correctness of the main vowel sound of each syllable for each word; (2) proper stress of the initial, internal and final consonants; (3) or, in some words, the right use of diphthong vowel sounds.

Since vowels give body and tone quality to words, it is vitally important that members be taught that every syllable of every word is composed of one of the following vowel sounds:

The Five Main Vowel Sounds
1. a (may)
2. ee (me)
3. ah (lot)
4. o (know)
5. ōō (too)

Variations of the Main Vowel Sounds
1. ih (sit)
2. eh (set)
3. aeh (sat)
4. ueh (turn)
5. aw (God)
6. uh (used especially when there is an "r" sound in a word)
7. ŏŏh (full)

Since consonants are necessary to give clarity to words, it is important to instruct choir members about these sounds as well. Consonants are classified in various ways. There are the explosives, so called because the current of air is completely stopped and then suddenly released. These explosives are further divided according to the place of stoppage of the air. They are:

Labials — p and b
Dentals — t and d
Palatals — ch and j
Gutturals — k and g (hard)

When the breath stream is only partly blocked, the consonants are called continuants. These are: l, r, m, n, ng, th, f, v, s, z, y, and sh. Continuants may be lengthened or sounded continuously, as the word implies, in contrast to the explosives, which are uttered quickly. Other classifications of consonants are as follows:

Bi-labial — consonants articulated by the two lips — p,b,m
Labio-dental — consonants formed by the lower lip against the upper teeth — f,v
Dental — consonants produced by the tip of the tongue against the teeth or the teeth ridge — t,d,n,th
Sibilant — consonants accompanied by a hissing sound — s,c,sh,ch,j

The two main organs for articulating consonants, then, are the tongue and the lips. Good diction techniques require training in the independent control of these organs. This independent control is necessary so that the movement of these organs does not interfere with the relaxed down jaw, which is always needed in order to maintain an open throat and full tone quality. Never should singers be allowed to "chew" their words in order to achieve diction.

In developing diction consciousness, it is good for a director occasionally to study a portion of a song with the choir and to point out the vowel and consonant sounds of each word or each syllable of each word that everyone should be singing.

Example — My Jesus I Love Thee

mAH-eegEE-sUH-sAH-eelAH-vthEE

My   Je - sus   I   Love Thee,

AH-eenO-oo thAH-oo AH-rtm AH-een

I   know   Thou   art   mine

f-AW-rthEE-AW-lth-AH-f-AH-lEE-s

For   Thee   all   the   fol - lies

UH - vs IH - n AH - eer EE - s AH - een

Of   sin   I   re - sign

It is a helpful technique when working on diction simply to have the choir speak the words of a song with exaggerated articulation. In order to impress upon choir members the need for good tongue and lip action, some directors like to use various tongue twisters, such expressions as: "tip of the tongue," "church chaps chirp chants cheerfully," "the teeth and the lips," "Peter Piper picked a peck of pickled peppers," etc. Another good diction technique is that of having singers say the words with an intense whisper.

There are several basic concepts regarding good diction that choir members should be taught. These are listed briefly as follows:

1. Prolong the main vowel sound as long as possible. At the last possible moment add the final consonant just before the next initial consonant is about to be sung.

2. Change from one vowel sound to another easily, keeping as much smoothness, intensity and uniform quality of tone as possible.

3. When there is an extended passage of rapid notes on the same vowel, add a slight "h" sound (aspirate) before each note to make for added clarity.

4. Be careful not to get a thin "twangy" tone quality in words that have the "r" sound — such words as "father," "earth," "world," etc. Rather, use the "uh" vowel sound, prolonging this vowel as long as possible before the final "r" is added by a final quick action of the tip of the tongue.

5. A diphthong is a union of two vowels forming a compound sound. It starts with one vowel and ends with another vowel sound. Treat the weaker part of the diphthong as a consonant by getting over it quickly, but sustain the main part of the sound.

    Examples of Diphthongs
    1. ee-u (you or tune)
    2. ah-oo (how)
    3. ah-ee (my)
    4. a-ee (pray)
    5. aw-ee (oil)

6. When the explosive consonants come at the end of a word which is the last word of a phrase, articulate with exaggerated emphasis. When these consonants appear in words within a phrase, articulate with enough emphasis to make the word clear, yet do not destroy the smoothness and flow between the vowel sounds.

7. When consonants appear in the middle of a word, they

should be allotted to the succeeding vowel sound in order to achieve greater smoothness. Example — "taken" is not sung as "tak-en" but rather "ta-ken."

8. When "n" and "m" consonants appear at the beginning of a word, such as "my," or within a word, "sinner," or at the end of a word, "mine," intensify and prolong these consonants slightly to make for added smoothness and glide between the words or between the vowel sounds within the word.

9. When a word ending with a consonant is followed by a word beginning with a vowel, as in the words "night is," the final consonant of the first word should be treated as the beginning consonant of the second word. Example — "nigh-tiz."

10. Words with two inner identical consonants should be treated as though there were only one. Example — "suffer" should be sung "suh-fuh . . r."

11. In such words as "listen," and "often," the "t" is silent.

12. Sing "thee" when the word "the" appears before a vowel or silent "h" sound. Sing "thuh" when it appears before a consonant.

13. Be careful not to emphasize the sibilant sounds as these make for exaggerated hissing sounds. Especially when holding a tone that ends with one of these consonants, guard against anticipating in the slightest these sounds.

14. Sing each initial consonant quickly. Don't slide up to the vowel. Try to sing the consonant on the same level as the vowel sound, or, if anything, have a feeling that the vowel sound is approached from the top.

A word of caution should be given about the possibility of an undue exaggeration of diction. Although this is certainly not the common fault with the average volunteer choir, yet there are directors who have made their choirs so conscious of this problem that their diction techniques become obvious to the listener. This style of singing is either showy or pedantic. Singers trained under this type of leadership usually try so hard to have good diction that their facial expressions take on unusual contortions. It must be emphasized that diction is never an end in itself but rather a mere tool for the purpose of conveying the sincere message and mood of the song to the listeners. With the exception of special effects, the basic principle of all music is always that of achieving a tone quality that has smoothness and flow between each of the sounds. In piano music this is known as the "legato touch." Instrumentalists speak of this principle as the "slur or phrase," while in singing this is known as developing a "line" to the voice. Since the idea of diction implies exactness of each individual sound, one can readily see that it is possible to achieve clear individual sounds and yet be lacking in the necessary smoothness or flow required of good singing. In other words, singers must have a horizontal concept of the words as well as a mere vertical concept. This "line" or flowing quality is achieved basically by developing the full resonance for each vowel sound and allowing this resonance to glide the voice from one sound to the next. This glide is also assisted by a slight intensifying of the continuant consonants when they occur, especially the l,r,m,n,ng,v, and z sounds.

F. *Lack of Proper Balance.* In working with a volunteer church choir, one soon realizes that there seldom is an ideal balance of voices. Theoretically, the proportion of women's voices should be about five sopranos to three altos with the same proportion of basses to tenors. A choir of thirty, then, would have ten sopranos, six altos, nine basses, and five tenors. To be practical, however, a director must learn to work with the voices at hand and gradually strive for the "ideal" balance.

Generally most church choirs will have an over-abundance of second sopranos, first altos and baritones, a shortage of low altos and basses, and an acute shortage of first sopranos and tenors. One of the basic answers when working with a volunteer choir where the balance of voices is out of proportion is to choose music that is suited to that particular group. This may mean that in the early stages of a new choir a director may have to content himself for some time with SAB music until such time as enough real tenors and basses are found or developed.

It is often true that many so-called baritones and second sopranos may possess far greater range potential than realized and with a little encouragement and vocal help can be developed into acceptable tenors, basses and altos. The problem of lack of first tenors is often solved by using a few low altos on this part. Although this will not give the same brilliance as the real tenor quality, nevertheless it does provide balance, and satisfactory results can be achieved this way. It should be cautioned, however, that most voice teachers are concerned about the effect this practice can have upon the altos' voices if they are kept on this part too long. These girls will fail to develop any upper register quality in their individual voices and hence will have unusually limited voice ranges.

Another answer to this problem of balance might be found

in rearranging the seating plan of the choir. Generally, choirs sit with the sopranos and altos in the front sections of the choir loft with the men in the rear. Most directors place the tenors behind the sopranos with the basses behind the altos. Some directors prefer the basses behind the sopranos and the altos in front of the tenors in order to have the outer and inner voice parts close to each other. However, any seating plan must be governed by results. If any voice part is especially weak, the director can change the conventional seating plans and place the weaker part nearer the front. For example, if the men are over-balanced by the women, this problem can be solved by placing them in the front row with the women in the rear of the loft.

The final adjustments, however, for achieving a fine balance of parts in the choir are in the hands of the director. He must be keenly sensitive to chords and balanced progressions, of quick adaptability in bringing out important voice parts and lines, and able to push back those of less importance. This ability requires a thorough musical and textual grasp of each song a director conducts.

G. *Ineffective Interpretation.* One of the most common practices of volunteer choirs is that of singing a song without effective interpretation. It is possible to develop fine tonal quality, musical exactness, correct diction, good dynamic levels, and yet lack the intangible quality of conviction in the singing.

Well-intended musical effects are often performed merely in a mechanical manner. Choir members have been instructed simply to mark their music and to sing certain portions of a song loud, soft, fast, slow, etc., without ever having a real understanding of the emotional purposes of such interpretations. If the interpretation of any sacred song is to make a spiritual impact upon an audience (and if it doesn't, the choir might just as well not sing), a director must in some way instill in each member the same understanding and emotional grasp that he has himself. It is good for a director to ask himself as well as the choir such questions as these about each song to be performed: "What is the over-all character and mood of this song?"; "What did these words mean to the author?"; "Whom are we supposed to be representing as the singers?"; "What effect should the message of this song have upon the listeners?" After the members have grasped this type of emotional concept of the song they are to sing, they must then be challenged to let themselves get completely into the mood of the song, despite any feelings of exaggeration and self-consciousness.

A good rehearsal technique in this matter of getting people to think of the emotional meaning of a song as well as to sing that song with musical correctness is to rehearse occasionally in opposites. For example, rehearse loud passages softly, soft passages loudly; fast passages slowly, slow passages in fast tempo; diminuendo passages with a crescendo, crescendo passages with a diminuendo; ritard passages with an accelerando, accelerando passages with a ritard, etc. The purpose of this procedure is to impress upon the singers the need for right interpretation by showing them the ridiculousness of singing words that naturally call for a certain interpretative treatment in an opposite manner. There are several other basic concepts regarding meaningful interpretation about which choir members should be informed. These are listed briefly as follows:

1. Be able to express in your own words the meaning and emotional connotations of all of the individual words in the song.
2. Be aware of the possibilities of contrasts between words, phrases or verses of a song. Make these contrasts apparent and meaningful.
3. Make repeated words or phrases intensify and emphasize the thought by use of contrasts — making the repetition louder, softer, faster, slower, more emphatic, etc., but never letting repetition result in monotony.
4. Connect the thoughts between words, phrases, and verses when there is a relationship.
5. Be aware of a phrase with a series of descriptive words or thoughts, making sure that each word or thought within the series adds to the total meaning of that phrase.
6. Give sensitive expressiveness to individual words that have particular color and meaning.
7. Be aware of the question-answer relationships found in many songs.
8. Make quotations apparent when they occur.
9. Anticipate the climaxes in a song and be ready to make them inspiring when they occur.
10. Don't let loud or fast passages become uncontrolled in tone quality or in steadiness of rhythm. Don't let soft passages become slow and lifeless. Loud singing does not necessarily mean fast singing; nor does soft singing necessarily mean slow singing. Soft singing actually requires more emphasis on bodily support, diction, intonation, etc., than does loud singing.

There are several general considerations that should be noted for the director himself. Basic, of course, is the re-emphasis of the truth that for any song a director conducts he must spend a great deal of study in grasping the musical and emotional possibilities of that song. He should devise his own methods for studying and marking his music so that when performing the song he can tell at a glance the highlights he wishes to convey. However, all of his interpretation should still be governed within the framework of style, traditions and good taste for that particular number. A conductor should never strive to be individualistic just for the sake of being different. This does not make for true sincerity in his conducting. Tempos must be set by the stylistic demands of the text and music, yet suited to the abilities of a particular group. Even the tone quality desired by a conductor will vary from song to song depending upon the style or mood of that song. For example, music of certain periods, such as the early polyphonic music of the sixteenth and seventeenth centuries, would demand an entirely different tone quality from a dramatic number of the nineteenth century. In the former type of numbers the tone quality should be straight and child-like, as free of vibrato as possible. In the latter, the tone quality should be much more intense. A director should be able to hear mentally from his choir the tone quality that will best interpret the number to be performed.

It should also be cautioned that it is possible for a director to over-interpret any song. To avoid this danger a conductor must have an over-all plan of interpretation for a song and relate the individual areas of interpretation to the total effect desired. This is generally known as "progressive interpretation." It means that a conductor does not do much rubato conducting in the early stages of a song but rather saves any marked changes in tempo or dynamics for the later stages of the number.

The suggestions offered in this chapter can be had in outline form in the booklet written and published by Kregels entitled *Pocket Guide for the Church Choir Member.* This booklet can serve as a helpful study for new choir members with limited musical background, as a handy reference for the more experienced members, or as an aid for the director who desires to teach the fundamentals of musical knowledge to his choir. The topics covered are classified under the following headings:

I.   Spiritual Concepts for a Church Choir Member
II.   Basic Music Review
III.   Suggestions for Improving One's Ability to Read Music
IV.   Vocal Helps
V.   Breathing
VI.   Physical Sensations Involved in Singing

III. Materials

Another of the all-important areas for a church music director is that of knowing a great deal of worthy sacred music for his choir to sing. Many churches take the easy way out and simply subscribe to a commercial program whereby a publisher supplies them with a new number for each service. Some choirs get into a rut of singing the same music year after year. Either of these procedures is usually uninspiring for both choir member and listener. A director must be willing to pay the price of spending many hours going through publishers' catalogues, examining new music, attending choral programs and workshops, talking to other choir directors to find the comparatively few numbers that are "just right" for his particular group. Only in this way will a director develop a knowledge of choral literature and cultivate a sincere enthusiasm for the music he presents to his choir and congregation.

A. *Criteria for Choosing New Music.* The following criteria are suggested as a basis for choosing new music:

1. Is the text worthy? Does it have a Scriptural, evangelical emphasis? Is the text in keeping with the doctrinal positions of the church?
2. Will the text have spiritual meaning as well as interest for the average listener? Is there a sufficient climax to the song?
3. Are the words simply stated yet stimulating enough to the imagination to place them above the level of the commonplace?
4. Is the textual repetition empty and meaningless or does it add intensity and emphasis to the message?
5. Is the music itself melodically, harmonically and structurally good?
6. Does the rhythm of the song fit the rhythm of the words? Is the rhythm free from "jazziness" and cheap sensational effects?
7. Is the music in the proper style of the composer or period from which it comes?
8. Is there a general, over-all union between the words and

the music with regard to mood, meaning, accents, stresses, climaxes, etc.?

9. Is the song technically fit for this particular group? Will the choir be able to sing it well? Will they enjoy singing this number? Will I be able to conduct it properly? Is this number appropriate for the occasion intended?

10. Is the accompaniment good? Does it add something to the singing or does it merely double the voices? Is it overly showy so that it distracts from the singing?

B. *Program Building.* The following suggestions are offered for preparing special music programs:

1. Strive to have a central, unifying theme throughout the program.

2. Within this framework of unity there still should be variety and contrasts of numbers, moods, styles of music, presentations, etc.

3. Plan and pray for the program so that it leaves the audience with a real spiritual impact — not just entertains them.

4. The end of each section of numbers as well as the end of the entire program must reach a sufficient climax.

5. The length of the entire program should not be over 1¼ to 1½ hours.

With the wealth of available sacred music, dating in time from the Renaissance to the present, it would be extremely difficult to prepare any kind of complete listing of mixed chorus music. The following is merely a representative listing of such forms of sacred music as gospel song arrangements, hymn arrangements and anthems, as well as a number of standard longer works that many church choirs perform especially for the Advent and Passion seasons. It might be added that many of these larger works have complete orchestrations available. If a full orchestration is not possible for these occasions, often stirring special effects can be had by using just a few instruments such as a string enemble, harp, chimes, trumpets, celeste, etc.

C. *Gospel Song and Hymn Arrangement Collections.*

Choral Praises compiled and arranged by Osbeck. Distributed by Kregel Publications.

Tabernacle Choir No. 1,2,3. Published by Hope Publishing Co.

Gospel Choir Classics 1,2,3. Published by Singspiration.

Favorite Choir Arrangements compiled by DeVos. Published by Singspiration.

The Choir Master Collection by Hughes. Published by Zondervan.

Zondervan's Choir Album by Hughes. Published by Zondervan.

Inspiring Choral Arrangements by Hughes. Published by Zondervan.
Choral-aires by Peterson. Published by Zondervan.
Choir Favorites. Published by Singspiration.
Don Hustad's Arrangements 1,2. Published by Hope Publishing Co.
Chorus Choir Voices. Published by Lillenas.
Clayton's Collection of Choir Melodies. Published by Gospel Songs, Inc.
Choral Album by Richard E. Gerig. Published by Ives Choir Library.
Song A Log. Published by Van Kampen.

    D. *Anthem Collections*

Collection of Favorite Anthems, Vol. I, II, III. Published by G. Schirmer.
Concord Anthem Book by Davidson and Foote. Published by E. C. Schirmer.
Master Choruses. Published by Ditson Publishing Co. (Has a book with just voice parts as well as a separate book for the accompaniments.)

    E. *25 Selected Anthems*

"Almighty God of Our Fathers" by James. Pub. Wood, No. 569.
"A Mighty Fortress Is Our God" by Mueller. Pub. G. Schirmer, No. 8179.
"Beautiful Savior" by Christiansen. Pub. Augsburg, No. 51.
"Be Thou Near Me Lord" by Morgan. Pub. Kjos, No. 5114.
"Consider the Lilies" by Scott. Pub. G. Schirmer, No. 9819.
"Create in Me a Clean Heart" by Mueller. Pub. G. Schirmer, No. 8682.
"God Is a Spirit" by Bennett. Pub. G. Schirmer, No. 2477.
"God Is the Light of the World" by Morgan. Pub. Wood, No. 653.
"Go Not Far From Me, O God" by Zingarelli. Pub. G. Schirmer, No. 4889.
"God So Loved the World" by Stainer. Pub. Ditson, No. 332-08621.
"Hear My Prayer" by James. Pub. G. Schirmer, No. 7739.
"I Walked Today Where Jesus Walked" by O'Hara. Pub. G. Schirmer, No. 8401.
"Jesus, Our Lord, We Adore Thee" by James. Pub. G. Schirmer, No. 8311.
"Let Mount Zion Rejoice" by Herbert. Pub. Lorenz. No. 71.
"Open Our Eyes" by McFarlane. Pub. G. Schirmer, No. 7275.
"Open the Gates of the Temple" by Knapp. Pub. C. Fischer, CM 6388.
"O Rejoice, Ye Christians, Loudly" by Bach. Pub. C. Fischer, CM 6600.

"Peace I Leave With You" by Roberts. Pub. G. Schirmer, No. 4471.
"Seek Ye the Lord" by Roberts. Pub. G. Schirmer, No. 3731.
"Thanks Be to God" arr. by Cain. Pub. Boosey-Hawkes, No. 1756.
"The Beatitudes" by Evans. Pub. Remick, No. 5-G1307.
"The King of Love My Shepherd Is" by Shelley. Pub. G. Schirmer, No. 3125.
"The Lord Is My Light" by Allitsen. Pub. Boosey-Hawkes, No. 1339.
"The Palms" by Faure. Pub. Lorenz, No. 916.
"There Is a Balm in Gilead" by Dawson. Pub. Music Press, No. 105.

    F. *Several of the Standard Cantatas and Longer Works*
         for Passion and Advent Seasons
     Christmas Oratorio by Bach.
     Christmas Oratorio by Saint-Saen.
     Crucifixion by Stainer.
     Eastertide by Protheroe.
     Holy City by Gaul.
     Magnificat by Bach.
     Messiah by Handel.
     Olivet to Calvary by Maunder.
     Seven Last Words by DuBois.
     When the Christ Child Came by Clokey.

ASSIGNMENTS

1. Discuss ways of starting a new adult choir in a church.
2. Discuss ways of reviving a church choir that has lost its enthusiasm. Point out various techniques that are helpful for any adult choir for maintaining interest throughout the entire year.
3. Discuss procedures and techniques for improving each of the following:
   a. A choir's sight reading ability.
   b. A choir's tone quality.
   c. A choir's blend.
   d. A choir's diction.
   e. A choir's balance.
   f. A choir's interpretation.
4. Discuss: "What constitutes good music for an evangelical church?"
5. Prepare a complete 1¼-1½ hour rehearsal for a thirty-voice senior choir.

ADDITIONAL READING

1. *Basic Principles of Singing* by Rice. Published by Abingdon Press.

2. *Building a Church Choir* by Wilson and Lyall. Published by Hall and McCreary Company.
3. *Choral Directing* by Davison. Published by Harvard University Press.
4. *Choral Director's Guide* by Neidig and Jennings. Published by Parker Publishing Company.
5. *Church Music Handbook* by Thayer. Published by Zondervan Publications.
6. *How to Organize and Direct the Church Choir* by Nordin. Published by Parker Publishing Company.
7. *Technique and Style in Choral Singing* by Howerton. Published by Carl Fischer Company.
8. *Techniques in Choral Conducting* by Jones. Published by Carl Fischer Company.
9. *The Choral Conductor's Handbook* by Ehret. Published by Edward B. Marks Music Company.
10. *The Training of a Church Choir* by Sydnor. Published by Abingdon Press.

❀   ❀   ❀

Familiar Quotes for Thought

"A choir poorly trained is worse than no choir at all."

Donald Kettering

"One of the essentials of a good conductor is to know what he wants, and to see that he gets it."

H. W. Richards

"Every great conductor is a great teacher."

Glenn Dillard Gunn

"A choir is as good as its director; seldom better, never worse."

J. Ashton

7 | INSTRUMENTAL PROGRAM

One of the areas of a total church music ministry that is generally given little attention in most churches is that of the instrumental program. Although church music directors agree that the music of the church is and should be primarily vocal, there is a growing interest in church orchestras, bands, instrumental ensembles, and instrumental accompaniments for choral anthems. Because music, instrumental music in particular, is given greater emphasis in our public schools today than ever before in the history of public education, church music directors are finding more and more instrumentalists who wish to continue their amateur playing upon completion of school. A challenging question indeed is how to use this talent, experience and desire to serve the church music program most effectively. There is also the distinct possibility that some fine Christian young person will catch the inspiration of music from his public school training and in turn can be counseled and challenged regarding a life of Christian service in the field of sacred music.

It is not the intent of this chapter to discuss in detail the technical knowledge and problems of an instrumental program. Generally the church choral director, with some basic instrumental experience, will be capable of leading such a group provided his conducting techniques are sound. A basic instrumental background would include an understanding of transposition problems of various instruments, the clefs in which instruments normally play and the limitations, peculiarities and best playing ranges of each instrument.

I. Strings

A. *Violins.* A non-transposing instrument; plays from the Treble Clef; a good playing range is from G below Middle C to high C, although it is actually possible to play an octave higher than this. The four strings are tuned in fifths, beginning with G below Middle C. A mute (Sordine), which may be used with a violin, subdues the vibrations and creates a mournful, mysterious effect. This can be especially useful with obligatos and soft accompaniments. Plucking the strings is known as "Pizzicato Playing." A tremolo is produced by a fast shaking of the bow.

B. *Violas.* A non-transposing instrument; generally plays from the Alto Clef, which locates Middle C on the third line. This clef is best suited to the compass of the instrument, ledger lines being seldom required. For extremely high passages the Treble Clef is also employed. The range is from C below Middle C to high C or even the E above this high C. The viola's longer and heavier strings are tuned a fifth lower than those of the violin.

C. *Cellos.* A non-transposing instrument; plays from the Bass Clef. The playing range is from low C below the Bass Clef to the A above the Treble Staff. The cello's four strings are tuned in fifths, one octave below the viola.

D. *Bass.* A transposing instrument since it sounds one octave lower than written. Plays from the Bass Clef. The four string bass is the instrument most commonly used and is tuned in fourths, starting with the E below the Bass Clef. The range of the bass is from this low E to second space A on the Treble Staff. (It will, of course, sound an octave lower than this.)

II. WOODWINDS AND REEDS

A. *Flutes.* A non-transposing instrument; is played by blowing across a hole in the side; the highest of all wind instruments with the exception of piccolos. The range is from Middle C to an octave above High C. Uses the Treble Clef.

B. *Piccolos.* A transposing instrument in that it sounds an octave higher than written. Uses the Treble Clef. The range is from D above Middle C to the B♭ above High C. (Will sound one octave higher.) The playing technique is basically the same as that of the flute. Occasionally one encounters D♭ piccolos. These will sound a minor 9th higher than written. However, the C piccolo is gaining in popularity and is steadily replacing the D♭ instrument.

C. *Oboes.* A non-transposing instrument. Uses the Treble Clef. The best range is from B♭ below Middle C to E above High C.

D. *English Horns.* A transposing instrument in that it sounds a Perfect 5th lower than its notation. Uses the Treble Clef. Has generally the same written range as the oboe. However, it will sound a 5th lower.

E. *Clarinets.* A transposing B♭ instrument. Will sound one whole tone lower than written. Uses the Treble Clef. The written range is from E below Middle C to the C above High C.

F. *Bassoons.* A non-transposing instrument. Generally is played from the Bass Clef, although the Tenor or Treble Clefs are used when necessary. The range is from the B♭ below the Bass Clef to the top space E on the Treble Clef. The parts can be interchanged with the cello.

G. *Saxophones.* Transposing instruments with the exception of the C Melody sax. Saxophones are made in the following sizes: Soprano B♭; Alto E♭; C Melody; Tenor B♭; Baritone E♭; Bass B♭. The written range for all is practically the same — B♭ below Middle C to the D above High C. All use the Treble Clef. The fingering on all saxophones is the same so that it is comparatively easy for a person to transfer from one to another. The Soprano sax in B♭ sounds a whole tone lower than written; the Alto sax is E♭, a Major 6th lower; the Tenor sax in B♭, a Major 9th lower; the Baritone sax in E♭, an octave and a Major 6th lower.

III. Brass

A. *French Horns.* A transposing instrument. When written in the Treble Clef sounds a Perfect 5th lower; in the Bass Clef, a Perfect 4th higher than written. Both Treble and Bass Clefs are used for notation. The written range of the French horn is from low C below the Bass Clef to a high C above the Treble Clef. A challenging instrument, especially difficult for one to begin on. Prospects for this instrument should be carefully selected.

B. *Trumpets or Cornets.* Transposing B♭ instruments. Use the Treble Clef. Will sound one whole step lower than written. The written range is from G below Middle C to a High C. May be muted by means of a pear-shaped device set in the bell.

C. *Baritones or Euphoniums.* Transposing B♭ instruments when played from the Treble Clef. Are pitched an octave below the trumpet and use practically the same techniques as do the trumpets. When read from the Bass Clef they are a non-transposing instrument.

D. *Trombones.* A B♭, non-transposing instrument when played from the Bass Clef. Most published music written in the Bass Clef. The range is from the E below the Bass Clef to a G above Middle C, with even the possibility of a B♭ above Middle C by experienced players.

E. *Tubas.* Non-transposing instruments even though they are made in several different keys — F, E♭, C and B♭. The majority of tubas, however, are pitched in E♭ and B♭. The range is from 4th line B below the Bass Clef to the F above Middle C. Uses the Bass Clef. Can be used interchangeably with the string bass parts.

The E♭ tuba in Bass Clef fingers the same as a cornet in Treble Clef with a key signature adjustment. This makes it possible to switch cornet players (who are usually too plentiful) to tuba when this is necessary for the sake of balance.

IV. PERCUSSION

This category includes pianos, celestas, drums, chimes, cymbals, gongs, triangles, xylophones, marimbas, vibraphones, castanets, tambourines. etc.

Any instrument which is set into vibration through being struck, either with a specially designed hammer, stick or piece of metal or through coming into contact with their like or with the hand is called a percussion instrument. These are further classified as either tuned percussion or untuned percussion. Tuned percussion, those which are capable of producing sounds of definite and intended pitch, include: piano, kettledrums, bells (tubular and orchestra), celesta, xylophone, marimba. Untuned percussion, those which are intended for giving off rhythmical and accelerating sounds, include: snare drum, bass drum, tambourine, triangle, cymbals, gong, castanets.

V. INSTRUMENTAL TERMS AND EXPRESSIONS

A church music director should be acquainted with the various terms and expressions used by instrumentalists. Some of these expressions include: "Cue Notes" — notes that are notated in small fashion in certain parts so that these instruments can play these notes if necessary — that is, when the instruments for which these notes are intended are either lacking or limited. "Slurred" or "Tongued Notes" — when tones are played either in a smooth, connected manner or with individual distinctiveness. "Concert Key" — to play in the same key as that used for the piano part "Score" — music.

VI. WAYS OF PROMOTING AND DEVELOPING AN INSTRUMENTAL PROGRAM

A church music director can begin an instrumental program in one of several ways. For example, a general invitation and public announcement can be made for all those who play instruments to play during the congregational singing at the evening services. This type of accompaniment for the singing adds a great deal of inspiration for these services. There is, of course, the problem of transposition for a number of these instrumentalists. Though many will be able to transpose as they play, it often is troublesome for the younger players. It is surprising, however, how quickly young players can learn transposition. It is also possible to buy hymnals that contain most of the songs orchestrated for various instruments. For example, the following hynmals now have accompanying orchestrated books:

> *Crowning Glory Hymnal.* Published by Zondervan.
> *Great Hymns of the Faith.* Published by Singspiration.
> *Hymns for the Instrumental Ensemble* by McCoy. Published by Broadman Press.
> *Praise and Worship Hymnal* by Stringfield-Johnson. Published by Lillenas.
> *Worship in Song* by Lane. Published by Lillenas.
> *Orchestral Favorite Hymns of Praise.* Published by Hope Publishing Company.

For congregational singing, the four parts of a hymn can be distributed as follows:

> 1st violins — melody and melody one octave higher
> 2nd violins — alto
> Cellos or bassoons — tenor or bass
> String bass or tuba — bass
> Flutes — melody or alto an octave higher than written
> 1st clarinets — melody
> 2nd clarinets — alto
> Oboes — melody
> 1st trumpet — melody
> 2nd trumpet — alto
> French horn — alto
> 1st trombone — tenor
> 2nd trombone — bass

Gradually a music director should try to develop this group of volunteer instrumentalists into a better organized group. This can be done by having special practice sessions to prepare for specific occasions. When the interest is then "ripe," this group can be encouraged to have regular weekly rehearsals. It might be that in the early stages of development this group would do well to content itself with merely playing hymns. Well-played hymns with slight variations can prove satisfactory for preludes, special numbers and offertory performances.

Another possible way to start the instrumental program is for the director to survey the instrumental talent in the church by first distributing a mimeographed questionnaire. This questionnaire should supply the answers to these questions: name of instrument played, experience, whether instrument is available for use, ability to read music, willingness to attend periodic rehearsals and services, and whether any extra instruments are available for others to use. After these results have been tabulated, the music director can send a letter of invitation to interested members who will make the most well-balanced group. In this type of group the music director should try to have the musical standards as high as possible so that individual members develop a pride in belonging to such a group.

A well-balanced orchestra should be built primarily around the strings. A good balance for a medium-sized church orchestra would be as follows:

6 — 1st violins	2 — trombones
3 — 2nd violins	3 — 1st clarinets
1 — viola	2 — 2nd clarinets
2 — cellos or bassoons	2 — flutes
1 — string bass or tuba	1 — oboe
2 or 3 — 1st cornets or trumpets	2 — saxophones
2 or 3 — 2nd cornets or trumpets	1 — piano
1 or 2 — French horns	

approximately 25–30 pieces

This type of balance is difficult to achieve, especially in the early stages of the orchestra's development. Usually there is an over-abundance of brass players rather than strings and wood-winds. If it is necessary to use a large number of brasses, one of the first considerations is to have each of the voice parts — soprano, alto, tenor, bass — represented by one or more of the brass instruments. In this way a brass choir is formed, independent of what other instruments are available. Such a group is complete as an ensemble, or it may provide a nucleus around which almost any combination of other instruments may be used. Cornets or trumpets are best fitted for the soprano and alto parts; trombones and baritones can play either tenor or bass parts; French horns or mellophones prefer alto parts; tubas are best suited to the bass part. If this group with its excessive power completely over-powers the other instruments, it may be necessary to have some of the brasses muted, although it must be cautioned that muting does affect the pitch of the instruments.

VII. REHEARSAL SUGGESTIONS

1. Though there should be a variety of flexibility within each rehearsal, a director will need to have a well-thought-out plan and structure in order to accomplish maximum results within the limited time possible. A typical one hour, pre-Sunday evening service rehearsal will generally include the following:

Prayer-Devotional Time

Warm-up and Tuning

(It is good to begin by playing a familiar hymn to get everyone together. This can then be followed by a brief initial tuning.)

Technique Drills — i.e. Scales, balanced choir progressions, etc. Whole tone scales are especially good for improving a group's intonation.

Practice the congregational hymns to be played in the immediate service.

Rehearse and refine the special number to be performed in the service — prelude, offertory, etc.

Sight read one or more special numbers for future use.

Check the tunings one more time.

Review one last time the special number to be played in the service.

(Instrumentalists must always feel completely confident about any number for performance.)

2. Have all rehearsal preparations completed before the players arrive — i.e. chairs and stands in place, music in folders, the order of the numbers to be rehearsed prominently displayed, etc.

3. Do all possible to rehearse and perform in tune. (a basic problem for many instrumentalists.) Will need to do several tunings throughout the rehearsal, since wind instruments change and become sharper as they get warmer. Check the tunings again just before the start of the service. Once the service (prelude) begins, however, no more tunings or warm-ups.

4. Allow enough space for the rehearsal area — approximately four feet between rows and about 2½ feet between chairs.

5. Experiment with different seating arrangements in order to achieve the most balanced sound with any particular group.

6. Provide a place for the players to store their instrument cases and belongings during the rehearsal and church service.

7. Allow a few minutes for a break between the rehearsal and the service — perhaps even light refreshments.

VIII. MISCELLANEOUS SUGGESTIONS

There are several other important considerations regarding the instrumental program that a director should know. These are listed briefly as follows:

1. In this, as well as in all of his endeavors, a director must have the complete cooperation and support of the pastor, music committee, and church board, with their full understanding this program will likely cost money to start. This initial expense will include orchestrated hymnals, a variety of special instrumental collections, folders, stands, etc.

2. When purchasing music for a newly organized church instrumental group, it is best to begin with, if possible, collections of music rather than individual copies.

3. A director should order enough music so that there is a minimum of one copy to a stand or a copy for every two players. For younger groups it is best to have a copy for every player so that they can practice at home.

4. The assistance of a faithful librarian is especially needful for an instrumental group. Since instrumental music is expensive, it must be carefully preserved.

5. The services of a competent pianist is needed — one who can read well and play confidently. (Just anyone will not do.)

6. The music director must be certain that the church piano is consistently tuned to 440 pitch.

7. As the instrumental program develops, it is good for a church to start laying plans for a junior orchestra/ensemble, composed of the beginning and younger players in the church.

8. As the instrumental program develops, it is a good idea to encourage the church to have a long range plan for purchasing church-owned instruments, especially the hard to carry instruments such as marimbas, string basses, etc.

9. A director should do all possible to encourage the more talented instrumentalists to keep up with their instruments by suggesting worthy sacred solos for them to practice and then by using them for special occasions. Smaller ensembles, such as brass trios, quartets or sextettes, string quartets, wood-wind ensembles, etc., should also be encouraged, helped with their choice of music, and used for appropriate occasions when ready to perform.

10. Since the services of a capable church organist are always difficult to obtain, a church music director should do all possible to get his church to have a long-range program for helping and encouraging worthy young pianists to study

organ. This can be done by providing financial help with lessons, free practice facilities, performance opportunities, etc.

IX. INSTRUMENTAL USES

Instruments can be used in many interesting, creative ways in a church music program:

1. Preludes, mini-concerts, choir processionals and recessionals.
2. Offertory specials.
3. Congregational singing accompaniment.
4. Entire concert programs as well as individual special numbers.
5. Accompaniments for musical dramas, cantatas, choral anthems.
6. As a feature of the Sunday School assembly sessions.
7. As an outreach to services/opportunities outside of the church.

Further, the instrumental program is an excellent way of engaging individuals, both young and old, who might not otherwise be engaged in church life.

X. MATERIALS

Although there are good sacred orchestral collections and individual numbers available as well as secular transcriptions of a devotional nature that are appropriate for church use, the problem of sacred instrumental materials is a much greater problem than it is for the church choral program. Especially is this true of hymn orchestrations that are easy to play yet attractively arranged for a church orchestra or band with average ability. The following is a suggested repertory of instrumental sacred music that can be used with a church orchestra.

A. Collections:
1. *Choice Chorales and Hymns* by Wienhorst. Published by Concordia.
2. *Easy Ensemble Music* by Hanson. Also, Ensemble Music for Church and School (more advanced). Published by Hope.
3. *Holiday Hymn Tune Instrumentals* by Yoder. Order directly from Dr. David Yoder, 9851 Sheldon Rd., Elk Grove, California 95624.

4. *Hymns for Instrumental Ensembles.* Volumes 1, 2. Published by Augsburg Publishing House.
5. *Hymns in Harmony.* Volumes 1, 2. Published by Rodeheaver.
6. *Hymn Tune Instrumentals* by Yoder. Order directly from Dr. David Yoder. (see above address).
7. *Instrumental Melodies.* Volumes 1, 2. Gospel Publishing House, Springfield, Mo.
8. *Rubank Sacred Orchestra Folio* by DeLamater. Published by Rubank Co.
9. *Sacred Selections for the Instrumental Choir* by McCoy. Published by Broadman.
10. *Sunday Symphony* (10 titles). Arr. by Mayfield. Published by Singspiration.

B. Miscellaneous Materials:
1. *Sacred Brass Quartets* by Frank Garlock. Published by Musical Ministries.
2. *For the Brass Ensemble* (3 packets of two hymn arrangements each) by DeCou. Published by Singspiration.
3. *Christmas in Brass* by Uber. Published by G. Schirmer.
4. *Easter Hymns for Brass* by Smith. Published by Broadman.
5. *Jerry Franks Dimensions in Brass,* arr. by Norris. Published by Volkwein Bros., Inc.
6. *Devotional Melodies* by Stringfield, arr. by Whitman. Published by Lillenas. (15 solos arranged for nearly every instrument.)

ASSIGNMENTS

1. Discuss ways of beginning and promoting an instrumental program in a church.
2. Discuss the problem of transposition as it applies to each instrument.
3. Write out the first verse of "My Jesus, I Love Thee" for a viola using the Alto Clef.
4. Write out the first verse of "My Jesus, I Love Thee" for a trumpet trio, keeping the piano part in the key of F.
5. Using the hymn, "My Jesus, I Love Thee," show which voice part each instrument in a church orchestra would play. State also the key each instrument would play if playing this hymn for the congregational singing.

ADDITIONAL READING AND HELP

1. *Brass Instruments in Church Services* by Ode. Published by Augsburg Publishing House.
2. *Instrumental Ensemble in the Church* by Trobian. Published by Abingdon Press.
3. *Instrumental Music and Christian Fellowship* by Bixler. Published by Henry Printing Co., Eugene, Oregon.
4. *Instrumental Music in the Church* by Sims. Published by the Sunday School Board of the Southern Baptist Convention.
5. *Instruments of the Orchestra* (a presentation kit for directors) by the J. W. Pepper Co., 4273 Wendell Dr., Atlanta, Georgia 30336.
6. *Strings and Things* by Posey. Published by Convention Press, Nashville, Tennessee.
7. *The Technique of Orchestration* by Kennan. Published by Prentice-Hall, Inc.

8 | OTHER MUSICAL GROUPS

There are many services in the average church which need special music periodically without necessarily using one of the regular church choirs. Such services include the prayer services, the special meetings, young people's meetings, ladies' and men's meetings, Sunday school sessions, etc. The Sunday evening services, hymnsings, services throughout the summer months also provide excellent opportunities for using special groups.

I. The Administration of This Program

An active music committee is an essential in the administration and development of a total church music program. In addition to the regular board members or members of the congregation delegated to this responsibility, this committee should include the pastor, music director or directors of the individual musical organizations, the organists and accompanists, a sponsor from each of the children's choirs, a representative from the Christian education committee, and the presidents from the teen-age and senior choirs. Some of the main responsibilities of this committee include:

1. A concern for the overall spiritual effectiveness of the entire church music program, including such areas as the music used in the Sunday services, the choice and use of songs used in the various departments of the Sunday school, youth departments, etc.

2. A concern for such matters as providing leadership and proper facilities for each of the musical organizations as well as obtaining song leaders and accompanists for the Sunday school departments and youth groups.

3. A concern for the condition of the physical equipment used in the music program — pianos, organ, hymnals, church owned instruments, etc.

4. The establishment of policies with respect to such items as the use of the church organ, the preparation of a yearly proposed music budget for the church board, and the planning of several social and recognition events for the various choirs.

In addition to the above responsibilities, the music committee should meet periodically with the music director to consider the musical potential within the congregation and to schedule the music for the various services of the church. These committee meetings should be held at least several times throughout the year. It would be good to have a meeting in the late summer to plan for all of the services through the first of the year; another meeting the first of the year to plan for all of the services through Easter; another meeting to plan from Easter to summer; and another meeting in the early summer to plan for the services throughout the summer months. Generally the music director will act as chairman of these committee meetings. As in any well organized committee meeting, there should always be a printed agenda of the various items of business to be discussed.

Once the music committee has surveyed the musical possibilities within the church and has set up a schedule for all of the services within a certain period, a letter should be sent to all of the various individuals involved in furnishing special music. This letter should give the service, date and time that the individual or his group is requested to participate. It should also be stated in the letter that the music director or accompanist will contact the participants and make arrangements to practice with them before the service. This type of planning does away with the usual last minute, frantic attempt to get special music and insures a much better quality of performance as well.

In addition to its various graded choirs and instrumental organizations, a church music program should also include such groups as:

Men's Groups — A male chorus
                A male quartet
Ladies' Groups — A ladies' chorus
                Trios and quartets
Soloists, duets and mixed quartets
Various instrumental ensembles

In organizing these smaller groups it is best to organize them so that all of the individuals are compatible with each other and within the same general age bracket.

II. MEN'S GROUPS

A singing group that generally has the most popular appeal in any church is a men's group. Even though the vocal quality may not be the best, there is usually something quite impressive to most people about a group of singing men.

In most churches a male chorus is a rather loosely organized group that does not practice regularly. It is usually called together for special occasions and services. The membership is open to all who like to sing, regardless of ability. The rehearsals are often held before the Sunday evening service or perhaps as part of the regular monthly men's meeting. Usually this type of group sings the "old chestnuts" with the music arranged in "barber-shop style," that is, with the melody or "lead" in the second tenor part. This makes it possible to place on the melody of the song all of the men who do nothing more than carry a tune. A few other voices on each of the other three parts will soon produce a fairly good male chorus sound.

When it is possible to have a more select group and more definite rehearsal times, much higher musical standards should be achieved. Better blend, balance and dynamics as well as a better caliber of music should be expected. For this type of group it generally sounds best to use music with the first tenor part carrying the melody. These same principles of better performance and music should also characterize the church male quartet. The following is a brief list of gospel song collections for male voices:

Sing Men, Vols. 1,2,3,4. Published by Singspiration.
Gospel Song Messages. Published by Rodeheaver.
Men's Voices. Published by Lillenas.
Coleman's Songs for Men. Published by Broadman Press.
Male Quartets 1,2. Published by Ives Music Press.
Songs for Men, Vols. 1,2. Published by Zondervan.
Quartets for Men. Published by Rodeheaver.
Lillenas Songs for Men. Published by Lillenas Publishing Co.
Radio Bible Class Quartet Favorites. Published by Singspiration.
Old Fashioned Revival Hour Songs. Published by Singspiration.

III. LADIES' GROUPS

A ladies' chorus is similar to a men's chorus. It generally is not a formally organized group but is used primarily for special occasions or services. Like the male chorus the membership is open to all ladies of the church, regardless of ability, who desire to sing. It is often true that in a church there are many individuals with good voices who are unable to sing with the regularity of the senior choir but who welcome occasional opportunities to sing with these special groups.

Since the rehearsal times are usually limited for such a group, the music must be arranged so that it is easily learned yet attractive enough to interest the singers and listeners. Even the simple two-part songs can be used effectively for such groups, especially when the second part is in the form of a counter-melody or descant. Here again the greatest number of ladies will sing the melody part with enough other ladies who can sing harmony carrying the second part to give reasonable balance. From this larger group smaller groups such as trios, quartets and sextettes can often be formed. These smaller groups should be able to sing a better quality of music and sing with a greater degree of skill and precision.

There are numerous fine gospel song collections that can be used effectively for solo, duet, trio and mixed quartet work. No attempt will be made in this book to list these various publications. This information can be had at any Christian bookstore. It is often possible to find many fine special numbers in various hymnals, especially in those no longer in popular use. From these various sources a music director should build his own collection of special numbers. A director must train himself to be continually looking for new and interesting songs that can be used with one of these special groups. If possible, it is good to have periodic voice classes for those especially interested in improving their singing as well as to prepare solos, smaller ensembles, etc.

IV. INSTRUMENTAL ENSEMBLES

Beautiful musical results can be achieved with various combinations of instruments. For example, with string instruments (violins, violas, cellos, bass), trios, quartets, quintets can be formed. Strings can also be used to good advantage with various combinations of woodwinds such as flutes, oboes and clarinets. Woodwind ensembles such as clarinet duets and trios, saxophone trios and quartets can also achieve beautiful effects. Trumpet trios, brass quartets (2 trumpets and 2 trombones), or brass sextettes (2 trumpets, baritone, French horn, trombone, and tuba) can add a great deal of inspiration to a service.

Directors interested in finding more interesting and challenging music for brass ensembles should send for a catalog to:

> Brass Player's Guide
> Robert King Music Co.
> 112A Main Street
> North Easton, MA 12356

Interesting string and wind ensemble arrangements are available through the:

Maranatha! Music Co.
P.O. Box 1396
Costa Mesa, CA 92626

For the woodwind choir, a collection *Suite for Woodwind Ensemble* by Anderson, published by Belwin Mills, is recommended.

ASSIGNMENTS

1. Discuss the factors involved in having a well organized music department in a church. Discuss the responsibilities of the music department to the church board, Sunday school, youth work, etc.
2. As church music director, prepare an agenda for a music committee meeting to be held at the beginning of a new choir season.
3. List five numbers that you feel a volunteer male chorus would enjoy singing.
4. List five numbers that you feel a volunteer ladies' chorus would enjoy singing.
5. Discuss the various combinations of instrumental ensembles that could be formed.

SUGGESTED READING

1. *Musical Ministries* by Pratt. Published by G. Schirmer.
2. *Music Levels in Christian Education* by Tovey. Published by Van Kampen Press.
3. *Steps Toward a Singing Church* by Kettring. Published by Westminster Press.
4. *The Singing Church* by Liemohn. Published by Wartburg Press.
5. *The Singing Church* by Phillips. Published by Faber & Faber, Ltd.

9 | THE RADIO MINISTRY

Within the past few years evangelicals have become increasingly aware of the possibilities of using the medium of radio in the proclamation of the Gospel in this country as well as on the foreign fields. Even on the local level it has become common practice for many evangelical churches to include some type of radio work as part of their total ministry. Progressive churches such as these realize the benefits of such an endeavor. For example:

1. In one broadcast the radio ministry gets the gospel message to a greater number of non-Christian people than are reached in numerous church services.
2. The radio ministry establishes the testimony and reputation of the church in the minds of the residents and newcomers in a community.
3. The radio ministry provides a spiritual ministry to many Christian people confined to their homes.
4. The radio ministry gives opportunity for the church personnel to use and develop their talents by taking part in the broadcasts.
5. The radio ministry increases the missionary interest of the congregation.

Even Christian leaders who do not have regular church broadcasts are often called upon to participate in a radio service. It is the purpose of this chapter to give Christian leaders some basic suggestions for effective radio production, with special emphasis on the musical portion of a program. Discussion will include the two main types of religious radio programs: the church service broadcast and the studio program.

I. Broadcasting a Regular Church Service

This type of broadcast requires less "programming" than does the studio broadcast. The church service broadcast begins with the assumption that there are already a number of listeners who

have a sympathetic interest and are tuned in for the express purpose of sharing as participants in the service.

There are, however, several basic suggestions that a Christian
leader should consider when making plans for a church service
broadcast:

1. For the very best pick-up, expert advice should be obtained
   from an acoustical engineer, quite possibly the engineer
   from a local radio station, regarding microphone placements for the choir, congregational singing, instruments,
   etc.

2. Avoid dead spots or long delays in the service. Move quickly from one activity to another.

3. Use the organ to cover up crowd noises such as rising,
   sitting, etc.

4. Avoid singing directly into the microphone when leading
   congregational singing.

5. Give more life and enthusiasm to the music than that used
   for a normal service. Congregational singing can sound
   especially dull on the air when it is allowed to drag.

6. Have a special announcement or activity for the radio audience during the time of the regular church announcements
   or during the offertory.

7. Increase the interest of the radio audience by occasional
   remarks referring pointedly to the specific audience before
   you or the occasion which has brought them together.

II. THE STUDIO BROADCAST

The gospel broadcaster should begin with the assumption that
a large portion of his audience will be not at all interested in the
broadcast, or at best mildly apathetic to his efforts. It is for this
reason that he must employ every legitimate device for achieving
audience appeal.

One of the most basic underlying principles of any radio production is that the broadcaster must have an intense desire to
make every second of the broadcast as attractive and meaningful as
possible. Further, the gospel broadcaster must be able to see beyond
the mere microphone and be able to visualize individuals within
the audience listening to his message. He must be able to project
himself by means of his imagination to the many diverse needs
represented by this audience. He must sensitize himself to the
general religious, intellectual and cultural backgrounds of his
probable audience. With this insight and understanding he must
prayerfully plan each broadcast so that the Holy Spirit through him
makes for maximum spiritual effectiveness.

A church planning to embark upon a studio broadcast ministry to its local community should first consider the following factors:

1. The spiritual objectives for the broadcast.
2. The type of program that will best achieve these objectives.
3. The facilities available for the broadcast.
4. The musical talent available for the broadcast.
5. The personnel available for writing the script for the broadcast.
6. The personnel available for announcing and speaking.

A. *The Spiritual Objectives for the Broadcast.* A church planning to engage in a radio ministry should first of all have a clearly defined objective for such an endeavor. There should be an understanding by all concerned as to whether this is to be primarily a program for the non-Christians, a Bible study for Christians, a program of encouragement for shut-ins, a general devotional program, a program to attract people to the church services, etc. Not only should there be a basic underlying objective for the radio ministry, but there should also be a definite objective for each individual broadcast as well. Both the pastor and music director should know and agree upon the purpose and theme for each broadcast so that each of their ministries can complement the other to that end.

B. *The Type of Program.* Once the spiritual objective for a radio ministry has been determined, the local church must then decide on the type of program that will best achieve this purpose.

The church board with the pastor and music director, or perhaps a special radio committee appointed by the board or elected by the congregation, should then come to a decision on such matters as:

1. The name and identifying theme for the program.
2. The general format of the program.
3. The length of the program.
4. The best time to broadcast the program.
5. The ratio in time of music to speaking.
6. Choice of a radio station whose listening audience is best suited to the objectives of the radio ministry.

C. *The Facilities for the Broadcast.* Many churches with a radio ministry find it more convenient to broadcast using their own facilities rather than to be dependent upon the use of the radio station studio. However, when a local church decides to use its own facilities, it must first consider the various physical requirements involved in broadcasting.

A proper room or auditorium is of utmost importance. It should be a room with the proper acoustical properties. It must be a room with sufficient space for a musical ensemble if this is to be used. For example, acoustical engineers generally recommend the ratio of 1,000 cubic feet of space for each musical unit. If an ensemble of eight voices with organ and piano is used, there should be a minimum of 10,000 cubic feet of space. An auditorium must also provide the proper balance in the reproduction of sound between bright, live sounds and acoustical properties that deaden sounds. Generally one must experiment a great deal with various microphone placements, use of such items as drapes, portable partitions, etc., to achieve the ideal balance.

Most church broadcasts today are tape recorded. This has numerous advantages over doing live performances. It takes the pressure off the performers since mistakes can easily be erased and corrected, tapes can be spliced or cut to perfect the timing of the program, and programs can be repeated when necessary. However, recording for a radio broadcast requires the use of a fine recorder. A regular home-type recorder is not adequate for radio use. Before buying a portable recorder for its radio ministry, a church should check carefully with the radio station personnel to obtain their advice on the make and type of machine that proves the most satisfactory. The cost of such a machine will generally run from $1,000.00 to $2,000.00. There is also the matter of a good microphone. Most experienced gospel broadcasters prefer a microphone like the RCA 77-D Uni-directional (only one responsive side) for a good focused pick-up. Such a microphone generally will cost from $100.00 to $200.00, with the truly top quality microphones running much higher than this.

D. *The Musical Talent for the Broadcast.* The average gospel broadcast generally has a ratio in time of ½ to ⅔ music to speaking. It is important, then, that only the very best musical talent be used. Not everyone will do for the radio ministry. It is felt that if acceptable talent is not available, it would be better to use recordings of good sacred artists. It is a wise plan for a music director to give a tryout to each singer before allowing him to participate in the broadcast. Voices that sound all right for live performances are often not acceptable for radio work. This is especially true of the highly dramatic voice or the voice with a great deal of vibrato.

A good organist and pianist are paramount for a successful broadcast. The ideal is when these musicians are flexible as well as accurate, have the ability to read and transpose music quickly, can play suitable background or mood music, can modulate smoothly, and are keenly sensitive to the needs of good "programming."

The size ensemble that most music directors consider ideal is a group from seven to fourteen voices. From this size ensemble almost any four-part choir number can be performed. Also, smaller groups such as quartets, trios, solos and duets can be easily formed. Most music directors feel that groups larger than twenty voices present too many problems of organization, maneuverability and diction. However, it should also be mentioned that with a larger group there are certain advantages. The leader is not so dependent upon any one person, a greater number of people are being trained, and a wider circle of interested people is gained for the radio ministry.

With regard to choosing music and developing musical talent for the radio broadcast, the following suggestions are offered:

1. Use established, well-known hymns and gospel songs.
2. Use songs that have real spiritual worth yet enough attractiveness to make for audience appeal. It is always best to use simpler arrangements and do them well than to try to use more complex arrangements and perform them "sloppily."
3. Keep the songs short, usually about two minutes in length. Generally two or possibly three verses of a song are enough. It is better to have a greater variety of numbers rather than to do fewer long numbers.
4. Perform songs with slightly more tempo than those used for live performances, never at the expense, however, of making a song sound "cheap" or frantic.
5. Keep the piano and organ introductions to a song brief. Generally the key for a song can be established while the song is introduced with speaking.
6. Strive for as much variety and contrast between numbers as possible. For example, use variety in the size of the performing groups (the complete ensemble followed by a solo or trio); variety in the use of color between voices (men's vs. ladies' voices); variety between the tempos of the songs (a 4/4 song followed by a 6/8); variety between key signatures of songs (a song in the key of C followed by a song in the key of A♭); variety between the moods of songs (praise song followed by a devotional song). With all of this variety, however, there still must be maintained a sense of unity to the entire program.
7. Use good instrumental music when possible. For example, use piano and organ together, solos or combinations of strings, woodwinds, brasses, etc. However, use only hymns and gospel songs that are familiar to the average listener.

8. Keep in mind that the understanding of words is of utmost importance in radio singing. Give even more emphasis to diction techniques for radio work than you do for live performance.

E. *Writing the Script.* Almost without exception, every radio broadcast should have a prepared script, since groping for words and using repetitious and meaningless expressions are "major sins" for good production. In many communities radio stations reserve the right to see and approve the script in advance of the broadcast.

The basic principles of script writing are clarity, color and simplicity. In writing for radio the emphasis should always be on the way words will sound when read. A good rule for script writing is to express the thought aloud first before attempting to write. Words must be written so that they will make for the greatest fluency when spoken. The writer should do all possible to avoid combinations of sounds that emphasize the explosive consonants — b,p,d,t, etc., since these sounds tend to "blast" the microphone when spoken. The sibilants, too, s,z,th,sh, etc., should be avoided in combinations since the high frequencies characteristic of these sounds tend to produce a whistling or hissing sound.

The script should be typed double spaced on paper that is as noiseless as possible. There should be enough copies for all key personnel — the pastor, music director, organist, pianist. The script should be marked so that important words are underlined, <u>like this</u>. Minor pauses should be marked with single marks (#) and major pauses with double marks (# #).

The writing of verbal introductions for musical numbers is known as the "continuity." This may also include the writing to set a particular mood for an activity or speaker to follow. The following are examples of possible approaches for writing continuity for a musical number:

1. Read a related portion of Scripture or a portion of the song.
2. Give a Scriptural thought or an explanation of a spiritual truth.
3. Cite an appropriate illustrative anecdote.
4. Use poetry.
5. "Paint" a word picture.
6. Give the story of the composer of the song or of an incident associated with the use of the song.
7. Have a straightforward, simple introduction.

A *Sample Script Form*

MUSIC: Theme — Ensemble start in "cold" in the key of C.

ANNOUNCER: (organ background) modulate to key of F behind announcement

    # (double space these lines of continuity) #

MUSIC: Ensemble — "Praise to the Lord" (key of F)

ANNOUNCER: (organ background — modulate to the key of E♭)

    Poem — "His Faithfulness" author unknown

    #   #

MUSIC: Soloist — Jane Smith — "Great Is Thy Faithfulness" (1 verse)

    Etc.

The following miscellaneous suggestions are offered for writing radio script:

1. Think the whole program through before writing anything.
2. Write in short, clear sentences.
3. Avoid words and theological expressions that the average listener will not understand. Avoid controversial subjects.
4. Make the writing intimate and personal.
5. Avoid general and trite expressions.
6. Write positively. Don't use the passive voice any more than necessary.
7. Plan your program so that you leave 30-40 seconds at the end for the local station announcements. For example, a 15 minute program should actually consume about 14 minutes 30 seconds.
8. Don't be overly flowery and effeminate. Keep in mind the male audience when writing.
9. Acknowledge authors, composers and sources of materials. It is wise to check with the local radio station regarding their policy on the use of copyright songs. For major stations and networks, music used must first be cleared by B.M.I. or A.S.C.A.P. Keep in mind that a copyright is effective for 28 years with the possibility of being renewed for another 47 years. Songs copyrighted after January 1, 1978, however, have a term of protection for the life of the author/composer plus an additional 50 years. After 75 years, however, any song becomes public domain.
10. It is a good plan to make a personal collection of poems, illustrations and anecdotes classified according to subject matter. The material chosen and used must have meaning and appeal to you personally before it can be effective to others.

11. Use a variety of words to express the same thought. Consult frequently such books as *English Snyonyms and Antonyms and Prepositions* by James C. Fernald, published by Funk and Wagnalls Co., N. Y.

F. *Announcing and Speaking.* The same principles of voice production that are necessary for effective public speaking before an actual audience (full resonance, voice modulation and variety, vocal flexibility and projection) are even more applicable in radio speaking. Before a "live" audience one can supplement his vocal abilities with gestures, facial expressions and general personality. In radio speaking the listener hears only a voice. It is imperative, therefore, that any radio speaker do his utmost to master these basic techniques of public speaking. Above all, a radio speaker must learn to cultivate the conversational tone and manner. There must be warmth and sincerity in the radio voice with that indefinable quality of "believability" about it. The manner of speaking should be that of a good friend speaking intimately to another friend. In radio speaking there is no place for the dramatic, "preacherish" tone quality or the manner of orating to a large audience.

The following miscellaneous suggestions are offered for effective radio speaking:

1. Have a factual and emotional grasp of the script. Be able to express the entire text in your own words.

2. Let the script stimulate and challenge you before you try to do the same to others.

3. Stand or sit approximately 12 inches to an arm's length from the microphone, depending on the quality of the voice, the type of microphone, the studio and other variables. Be close enough to get intimacy but not so close as to sound "blasty."

4. Talk distinctly but not with an over precision that makes you sound stilted and artificial.

5. Practice reading a great deal aloud to achieve fluency. Especially is this necessary in the use of Bible names and expressions.

6. Be "time" conscious when reading. Gauge the length of your script by the normal rate of speaking, which is from 125-150 words per minute.

7. Be careful of mispronounced words. When in doubt, check a good dictionary. Other good books to have are: *25,000 Words Frequently Mispronounced* by Frank H. Vizetelly, published by Funk and Wagnalls Co., and the *NBC Handbook of Pronunciation.*

8. Avoid any of the following:
   a. Crumpling the pages of the script.
   b. Making vocal sounds such as clearing the throat or coughing.
   c. Moving around and about the microphone once the speaking begins.
   d. Touching the microphone during the speaking.
   e. Talking or making any sound at the conclusion of the program until certain that you are off the air.

ASSIGNMENTS

1. Discuss the spiritual possibilities for an effective church radio ministry in a local community. What are some of the problems that a church must face in starting a radio broadcast?
2. Discuss the various leading religious broadcasts on the air. Which ones appeal to you and why? Which ones do you feel are the most effective in reaching non-Christians with the Gospel?
3. What do you consider to be the greatest weakness of most religious broadcasts?
4. Choose ten songs that you feel are appropriate for a radio broadcast. Pick two verses from each hymn, justifying your choice of these songs and verses.
5. Prepare a fifteen minute devotional broadcast. Write a script, showing the theme, the musical numbers to be used, the continuity, the length of the message, etc.

SUGGESTED READING

1. *Handbook of Broadcast* by Abbott. Published by McGraw-Hill Co.
2. *Manual of Gospel Broadcasting* by Loveless. Published by Moody Press.
3. *Psychology of Radio* by Cantril and Allport. Published by Harper Co.
4. *The Church in the World of Radio-Television* by Bachman. Published by Association Press.
5. *The Modern Broadcaster* by Lawton. Published by Harper Bros.
6. *Broadcasting in America* by Head. Published by Houghton-Mifflin Co.
7. *Fundamentals of Radio Broadcasting* by John Hasling. Published by McGraw-Hill Co.

10 | THE WORSHIP SERVICE

It has become a custom in evangelical churches for the Sunday morning service to be considered the worship service with the evening service given an evangelistic emphasis. This order may be changed in some instances depending upon local circumstances. For example, if it is felt that more non-Christians are attending the morning service, the church's leadership may feel inclined to give this service more evangelistic emphasis and make the evening service a worship service for Christians. Regardless of the hour chosen for the services, the Christian church has a twofold function to perform: That of leading and instructing believers in their worship of God and that of witnessing to those who are unsaved. Neither responsibility should be neglected. It must be admitted, however, that in many of our evangelical churches our desire to see people reached with the gospel message has resulted in almost every church service being an evangelistic type of service. There is real danger that Christians in such churches receive little instruction in the Word of God for a growth in grace and in the "graces" for their individual lives.

Since an evangelical church has no prescribed order of worship as in the more liturgical churches, it becomes the responsibility of each local pastor and music director to prepare a spiritual and mature order of activities for each worship service. However, before any Christian leader can properly plan such a service, he must have a clear and positive understanding of the meaning and importance of worship. The word "worship" is a contraction of an old expression in the English language, "woerth-scipe," denoting the ascription of reverence to an object of superlative worth. A more theological definition of worship is given as follows: "An act by a redeemed man, the creature, toward God, his Creator, whereby his will, intellect and emotions gratefully respond to the revelation of God's person expressed in the redemptive work of Jesus Christ, as the Holy Spirit illuminates God's written Word to his heart."

177

The act of worship, then, implies communion and fellowship: The eternal, infinite God deigning yet desiring communion with man; and finite man in turn capable of approaching and fellowshipping with Almighty God.

The portion of Scripture that presents the most complete teaching of the New Testament principles of worship is found in the fourth chapter of the gospel of John. Here the Lord confronted a lowly woman from Sychar of Samaria with the most important issues of life: First, an invitation to find the "living waters" that alone could provide eternal satisfaction for her longing heart; then, following the woman's salvation experience, the Lord taught her the meaning of worship. The result was that "many of the Samaritans of that city believed on Him for the saying of the woman, which testified, 'He told me all that ever I did.'" This, then, is always God's divine pattern for any individual: salvation, worship, service.

I. OLD TESTAMENT WORSHIP

To understand the full import of the lesson about worship that Christ taught the woman of Sychar, it is necessary to review some of the important principles and traditions of the Jewish religion, the direct ancestor of Christianity.

The worship of Jehovah for the Israelites was always associated with a particular place and had a special ritual. After traveling through the wilderness for some months, the Israelites were given the laws of God, tables engraved with the Ten Commandments. In order to keep these tables safe, God directed Moses to take an ark of acacia wood overlaid with pure gold within and without. There were gold rings at each corner, through which went long poles of acacia wood covered with gold for carrying purposes. The lid of the ark was of solid gold and was called the mercy seat. At each end were cherubims of gold facing one another, as their wings came out over the mercy seat like a tent. God made a covenant with the children of Israel and said: "And there I will meet with thee, and I will commune with thee from above the mercy seat, from between the two cherubims which are upon the ark of the testimony" (Exodus 25:22). Thus, the ark and the mercy seat constituted the place of worship where God and man could meet together and enjoy sweet communion with each other.

The first building in which Israel worshiped was a tent called the Tabernacle. This "tent of meeting" was built as a result of God's direct command: "Let them make me a sanctuary; that I may dwell among them" (Exodus 25:8). God gave Moses specific instructions for the construction of this building. It had to face east, was to be

45 feet long, 15 feet wide, 15 feet high, and constructed of particular linen curtains, skins, boards and other materials. Every detail for the arrangement of the interior of the Tabernacle was also specifically prescribed. This included the placement of the shewbread, the candlestick, the brazen altar, the altar of incense and the laver.

With the capture of Jerusalem under David and the permanent establishment of the Tabernacle in that city, the worship ritual became increasingly important. With the building of the first temple under Solomon, David's son, and still later the building of the second temple following the Babylonian captivity, the worship service continued to be an extremely elaborate and ritualistic affair.

II. NEW TESTAMENT WORSHIP

The type of worship that Christ taught the woman from Sychar, therefore, was a startling new concept of worship for the people of her day. It was a worship based on personal sincerity and simplicity rather than on tradition and ritual. Since God is a Spirit, He must be worshiped by the corresponding faculty in man. Worship as taught by Christ had to be a personal soul expression, an inward attitude rather than a physical or tangible act. In the Old Testament man's worship was commanded by God. In the New Testament man worships because he desires to fulfill the Father's will. In the Old Testament man could only approach God through the prescribed rituals of the Temple. In the New Testament an individual's relationship to God is immediate and personal.

In the Biblical account of the woman at the well there are other theological implications that are basic tenets of the evangelical position. First, there is the truth of the priesthood of the individual believer. Every believer, whether he be clergy or laity, is in the same status before God (I Peter 2:5, 9; Revelation 1:6). The fact that this new concept was revealed to a lowly Samaritan woman rather than to the religious leaders in the Temple and synagogues gives evidence of this. Further, we are taught that our worship is not associated with or limited to a particular place or ritual, but rather that each believer is the temple of God (I Corinthians 3:16). Moreover, the only sacrifices that God requires today are the spiritual sacrifices of each believer (Romans 12:1).

The realization of these New Testament truths had a stimulating effect upon the early Christians. Despite the opposition and suppression of their worship by Roman soldiers, nothing could stop their witness for Christ. Everywhere they were known for their joy and steadfastness. Acts 2:42 reveals that the infant church after Pentecost "continued stedfastly in the apostles' doctrine and fellowship, and in the breaking of bread, and in prayers."

With the legalizing of Christianity under Constantine the Great in 313 A.D., the simple organization of the apostolic church gradually developed into a complex system of liturgy and ritual. The clergy were no longer the servants or representatives of the people but held a mediatorial position as the channels through which divine grace was transmitted to the faithful. By the seventh century the ritual of the Mass as practiced in Roman Catholic churches today was established. The twelfth century saw a further decline in the individual's participation in worship as congregational singing was for the most part discontinued. The meaningless ritualism and lack of individual participation in worship were among the factors that led to the Reformation of the sixteenth century. Martin Luther strongly contended that the service belonged to the people and that worship should be the grateful response from every believer's heart. The use of the Latin language was discontinued by Luther and congregational singing was once again restored to its rightful place in the worship of God.

III. CORPORATE WORSHIP

Not only should worship be practiced daily in each believer's private devotional life, but as Christians we are commanded to "consider one another to provoke unto love and to good works: Not forsaking the assembling of ourselves together, as the manner of some is; but exhorting one another: and so much the more, as ye see the day approaching" (Hebrews 10:24, 25). This group or corporate worship has the promise of the Lord that "where two or three are gathered together in my name, there am I in the midst of them" (Matthew 18:20).

The term "liturgy" is commonly associated with group worship. This word comes from two Greek words, *leitos*, which means "public," and *ergon*, which means "service." The evangelical use of this word implies simply the order of service or the arrangement of the various items that are employed in any public service. This, then, distinguishes a liturgy from a ritual since a ritual is set and unvaried, while an order of service for an evangelical church can be arranged in any number of ways. For the evangelical, the term "worship" when applied to corporate worship is an all inclusive term including all of the activities in a service such as: expressions of praise in song, Scripture readings, prayers, the offering, the Lord's Supper, and the preaching and instruction from the Word of God.

There are varying degrees of emphasis on liturgy in churches today. There are those in the highly liturgical churches who believe that their liturgy is divinely inspired and that those who are faithful in sharing this means of grace eventually will receive their just reward. There are other church groups that place a great deal of emphasis upon the aesthetic and cultural factors associated with worship. The main objective of these churches is to achieve the "beauty of holiness." Such items as church architecture, furnishings and the general formality of the service all become of paramount importance. There are other churches that emphasize the psychological benefits that come to an individual as a result of a worship experience. These churches teach that as an individual comes under the calm and tranquilizing influence of the worship service, he in turn will be able to live a worthier life. There are other churches that are strongly reactionary and opposed to any form or liturgy in their worship, believing that a service should be completely spontaneous since this is the only way the Holy Spirit can lead and direct.

The evangelical concept of worship differs from all of these views. The evangelical believes that a liturgy must be flexible so that it can be adapted to each local situation and best meet the spiritual needs of a particular group of people. Further, the evangelical believes that beauty and dignity have their place as aids to worship but should never become the objects of worship. Surely, however, the building dedicated for the worship of God should be at least as clean, attractive and appropriate for its purpose as the house we desire for our daily living. The evangelical also believes that there is personal benefit to those who attend church, but he qualifies this by saying that only those who know God through a personal faith in Jesus Christ can worship properly and thus know the true peace of God in their lives. Finally, the evangelical, too, keenly desires spiritual reality and meaning in every item of the service but believes this can be accomplished in an appropriate and mature manner. He is convinced that the Holy Spirit can lead one in the preparation of a service as well as He can inspire in a spontaneous manner.

There need be no undue emphasis or fear of such terms as "form," "dignity," or "reverence" as applied to a worship service. It is well, however, to distinguish clearly between "form" and "formalism" when discussing a liturgy for a worship service. "Formalism" implies pretense, deadness, ritual and pageantry. This was the type of worship for which Christ strongly rebuked the Pharisees (Matthew 15:8, 9). "Form" simply implies an act or behavior that is appropriate for a particular situation. For example, even in the matter of one's own dress, there is appropriate clothing for various types of activities. Certainly one would not dress for participation in some sports event in the same way he would for a formal occasion. However, it would be possible to be dressed appropriately for an occasion and yet arrive physically unfit for participation. Appropriateness with reality, then, is form; pretense and deadness are the characteristics of formalism and ritual. This is a danger against which every evangelical leader must constantly guard.

Worship flourishes best in the atmosphere of freedom. "Where the Spirit of the Lord is, there is liberty" (II Corinthians 3:17). Freedom of Spirit, however, does not mean haphazardness, irregularity and fanatical confusion. While worship is spiritual and not formal, the spiritual worship of any assembly will naturally assume some outward form, since it is impossible to have any group activity without that group being agreed as to a way of doing things together. It is through an appropriate form that unity of thought, feeling and purpose are best secured. It should be pointed out that in a simple or informal service a type of formalism can develop that is just as deadly as the most complicated ritualistic service. The trouble, then, does not necessarily lie with the form, but with those who use it.

The New Testament does not give any definite or specific instructions as to a proper form for a worship service. There are, however, certain general principles that can be learned from several portions of Scripture. Foremost is the Apostle Paul's exhortation to the church of Corinth to do all things decently and in order (I Corinthians 14:26, 33, 40). He further contended for reality in every spiritual activity, rebuking the wrong use of such gifts as prophesying and speaking in tongues. He stated that he would rather speak a few words with clarity than to utter much that was unintelligible. The Apostle Paul also implied in his instructions to Timothy a conduct that was appropriate for an individual when the church of the living God, any group of believers, assembled for worship: "That thou mayest know how thou oughtest to behave thyself in the house of God, which is the church of the living God, the pillar and ground of the truth" (I Timothy 3:15).

IV. THE APPROACH TO WORSHIP

An individual's general attitude of worship is largely determined by his concept of the Godhead he is worshiping. If one realizes the true attributes of God the Father — His being, character and works, he will approach Him with the proper recognition of His worth. If, however, God is no bigger than an individual's personal needs and experiences, the approach to God will be more self-centered and less worshipful. This is much like the relationship of a child to his parents. Until a child reaches maturity, his main devotion to his parents is primarily in terms of what they can and will do for him. Later, however, he begins to see his parents in a new way. He recognizes qualities in his parents that make him appreciate them simply for what they are themselves. Spiritual maturity, too, requires this kind of recognition of God. It is for this reason that every worship service should include the singing of hymns and expressions of praise solely in worship and adoration of God for who and what He is. This is generally spoken of as the objective approach to worship.

A leader of a worship service must not only lead his people into the presence of God the Father and thereby develop in them a realization of the greatness of God, but he must also quicken in them an awareness and appreciation of their personal salvation, since the Christian revelation of God is only fully realized in the redemptive work of Jesus Christ. This is what gives worship warmth and vitality. This is generally spoken of as the subjective approach to worship.

It is also necessary to recognize the ministry of God the Holy Spirit in our worship. When there is an absence of the Holy Spirit and His illumination of the Word of God in individual hearts, formalism and meaningless action result. Each person of the Trinity, then, is worthy of our adoration and praise: the Father as the object of our worship; the work of Christ as the basis of our approach to God; and the ministry of the Holy Spirit in illuminating and motivating our worship.

A right approach to worship by each worshiper should naturally result in proper decorum in a worship service. This would mean that a worship service should be characterized by such attitudes as reverence, sincerity, humility and dignity. Such actions as whispering, lack of attentiveness, reading of Sunday school papers and gum chewing should have no place in a worship service. A service should be filled with inspiration, praise and thanksgiving. Congregational singing should always be the chief expression of a group's praise of God. There should be a restful, meditative atmosphere, where people can hear God's "still small whisper." There should be an attitude of eagerness to receive instruction from God's Word. Finally, the service should be challenging. The climax of a service should be the subjecting of the human will to the divine will. Every service of worship should give opportunity for such a response on the part of the people to all they have thought, heard and learned of God. A worship service should stimulate and motivate worthier discipleship and more dynamic crusading for Christ in each believer in his own areas of activity and influence.

V. SUGGESTIONS FOR IMPROVING A WORSHIP SERVICE

It has well been said that proper attitudes are better "caught" than "taught." It is especially important, therefore, that any leader who attempts to lead others in a proper attitude of worship must first set a good example before his people. A leader's manner should be warm and sincere, yet mature and dignified. He should treat the group as participants rather than as mere spectators. It has been suggested that a leader's manner in bringing his people into the presence of God should be that of introducing one respected friend to another such friend. Leaders who display careless or gaudy dress, undignified speech, foolishness, flippancy or haughtiness, will definitely hinder a proper worshipful attitude in a group. Not only must a leader set the proper example, but there are times when it may be necessary to deal more directly with conduct that is unbecoming in the worship of God. This can be done by devoting a message to the subject of worship or by having reminders in the bulletin or the foyer of the church. A tactful way of handling this problem is to bring a series of short children's talks as part of a regular service, dealing with the subject of "How We Behave Ourselves in Church." In this way children learn these ideals early in life, and the older members of the congregation as well can learn and relearn these lessons in a way that does not seem directly pointed at them.

There are several basic truths regarding a proper attitude for worship that a leader should try to teach a congregation. First, worship requires preparation. This spiritual preparation should begin in the home before the family arrives in church. Upon arriving in church there should be the further preparation of silently asking God's blessing upon the service. In other words, a spiritual attitude of worship cannot be turned off and on like a faucet. Further, believers must be taught that a proper attitude of worship requires willful concentration and self-discipline while in the service so that nothing is allowed to distract from their worship of God. It has become increasingly true in many of our evangelical churches that an attitude of going to church simply to hear the preacher or the music — to be entertained — has developed rather than a spiritual attitude of sincerely desiring to worship God. Then, Christians should be taught that they should be active participants rather than mere spectators during each activity of the service. This means that they should share wholeheartedly in the singing, enjoying and appropriating the truths of the songs they sing. They should be made to realize that even when listening to the Scripture readings, pastoral prayers, special music, message, etc., they can be sharing vicariously in these activities as well. The offering, too, is an act of worship. People should be taught that the offering is not merely collecting enough money to meet the financial obligations of the church. In a far deeper sense the material gifts should be a symbol of one's spiritual attitude — that of love, devotion and commitment to Christ. This entire matter of definite and genuine participation on the part of the congregation is one of the basic principles of evangelical worship.

A leader of a worship service should strive to keep a proper balance between the objective and subjective approaches to worship. Both are needed. Generally, most leaders think of the service as being objective until the time of the Scripture reading, after which the service gradually becomes more subjective. There must also be a proper balance between having enough routine in a service to give stability and enough variety to give interest. The result of stability and habit alone is mechanical repetition while too much variety soon develops into mere entertainment. A service should, in addition, have unity. This does not mean that an entire service must be built around a common theme such as the message, since the service has different moods and varied emphases which must appeal to many different individuals with diverse ages, needs, temperaments and backgrounds. Rather, the unity in a service is sometimes compared to the playing of a symphony with its contrasting sections, themes and moods, but all contributing to one total impression. A service also demands movement. Feelings and emotions, like a stream of water, are powerful only as they keep moving. Finally, a service must give evidence of preparation and thought even to minute details. An audience does not like to be part of a service when it senses a leader's insecurity and disorganization.

There is no one way to arrange the various items for a worship service. However, many leaders recommend Isaiah's vision of God and his call to service as recorded in the sixth chapter of Isaiah as the ideal order for a worship service. From this Biblical account, Ilion T. Jones in his book, *A Historical Approach to Evangelical Worship*, suggests the following list as the basic needs of worshipers to be satisfied by the service:[1]

---

[1] Ilion T. Jones, *A Historical Approach to Evangelical Worship* (New York: Abingdon Press, 1954), p. 267.

1. Vision of God: adoration, sense of His presence
2. Confession: humility, penitence, contrition, repentance
3. Forgiveness: relief, release, cleansing, assurance of pardon
4. Thanksgiving and praise
5. Joy: comfort, exaltation and exultation
6. Fellowship: sense of common or corporate bonds
7. Instruction: illumination, insight
8. Dedication: sacrifice, offering
9. Call: ethical demands, inspiration, stimulation to action

Most worship services begin with an organ prelude. If an organ or a capable organist is not available, it is suggested that a church use good organ recordings for this purpose. A worthy, devotional prelude is most important to a worship service since it provides a meditative atmosphere as people arrive, thus establishing the proper mood and attitude for the entire service. A call to worship by either the choir or pastor, or often both, is usually the next item. There are a number of suitable hymns or responses that a choir can use for this choral call to worship or "Introit" as it is sometimes known. A pastor can use portions of any number of various Scriptures that are appropriate, with the Psalms offering perhaps the greatest treasury of such verses. Other possibilities for the call to worship by the pastor include the use of sacred verse or portions of hymns. It is advisable for a pastor to make a collection of suitable materials for this purpose. After the call to worship there is usually some group singing, such as the Doxology, Gloria Patri, or an opening hymn. Other activities such as the invocation, special music, responsive readings, Scripture readings, pastoral prayer, choir responses, offering, more congregational singing, message, closing hymn, benediction and postlude are included in most worship services. The closing benediction is generally given from one of the following: II Cor. 13:14; Eph. 3:20, 21; Num. 6:24-26.

In many churches other items of worship are included, such as processionals and recessionals, both Old and New Testament Scripture lessons, organ interludes, the Lord's Prayer, silent prayer, the reading of the Law (The Decalogue), an affirmation of faith such as the Apostle's Creed. However, it should be emphasized again that elaborateness is not the goal in worship. In fact, it should be cautioned that church history has proven that usually the decline of real fervor and spiritual force in the church is preceded by a craving for elaborate ritual and pageantry. The goal of an evangelical church must always be that of realizing spiritual reality in every item in the service so that hearts are properly prepared for the ministry from God's Holy Word. A simple form of service in a small rural church, then, can be just as worshipful as any other.

Since in worship services considerable time is concerned with musical activities, it is vitally important for every church music director to give prayerful consideration to these matters of worship. He must work in close cooperation with his pastor in planning an effective service for his congregation. It is generally agreed by Christian leaders that there is no better medium for expressing group worship than congregational singing. The choice and use of the congregational songs, then, becomes as serious a matter as the choice of the sermon topic. The following suggestions are offered:

1. Use three congregational songs before the message.
2. The opening song should be a hymn, objective in content — the praise of God, His majesty, etc. The use of the personal pronouns should not be emphasized. Rather, the emphasis should be upon God. The melody, harmony and rhythm of the song should also be worshipful. This hymn should be one that is generally familiar to the congregation. Example — "All Hail the Power of Jesus' Name."
3. The second song can be more subjective in content, one that extols the redemptive work of Christ, or speaks of devotion and love to the Saviour. Example — "My Jesus, I Love Thee."
4. The congregational song before the message should be one that prepares hearts for the spoken word — asking the Holy Spirit's illumination, etc. Example — "Holy Ghost, With Light Divine."
5. The congregational song after the message should be one that reinforces the truths of the message and challenges believers to appropriate the truths they have learned. Example — "Take the Name of Jesus With You."
6. Songs should be Biblically sound as well as singable for a congregation. Often songs that are excellent for choirs and smaller groups do not lend themselves to congregational use.
7. The music as well as the words must be considered when choosing songs. Special consideration must be given to the melody and rhythm of a song. A tune should reinforce the spirit and emotional meanings of the words. It should correspond with the words by having the same accents and stresses as the words. The most important words should be the longest notes, highest pitches, etc. Rhythms, too, must correspond with the spiritual emphasis of the words. Rhythms that are syncopated, lilting and secular in connotation have no place in the worship of God.

The choir should take an active role in the leadership of a worship service rather than only provide a special number. This practice can easily degenerate into mere entertainment for the congregation. Individually, choir members must be impressed with the fact that they are to be leaders of the service — leaders of congregational singing, responsive readings, etc. The use of appropriate choir responses throughout the service — the call to worship, pastoral prayer, offertory and closing responses — can add a great deal to the spirit of worship in a service. The evangelical principles of simplicity with spiritual reality can be applied here as well. For example, in the well-known hymn, "My Faith Looks Up to Thee," there is the refrain:

> "Now hear me while I pray, take all my guilt away;
> O let me from this day be wholly thine."

This response can be just as effective in maintaining an attitude of prayer after a pastoral prayer as a more complicated and liturgical response. There are numerous other short hymns or refrains from longer hymns that can be used for this purpose. As previously mentioned, there are a number of suitable hymns that can be used for the choral call to worship. All of these choir responses should be varied often so that they do not become mechanical and routine. The words of a response must always be meaningful, pertinent and generally familiar.

In closing, the importance of such matters as proper room temperature and ventilation should also be mentioned. Attractively printed bulletins are also helpful. These should be complete in their information so that verbal announcements are kept to an absolute minimum. It is also important that there be a plentiful supply of hymnals for everyone. Good ushering, too, plays an important role in the success of group worship. Ushers should be instructed in such matters as:

1. The importance of a cordial greeting to everyone.
2. An awareness of visitors — making them feel welcomed, etc.
3. The proper procedures for directing people to their seats.
4. The matter of seating late-comers at the proper time. Fitting them into the service by informing them of the song being sung, etc.

It is recommended that each usher be given a copy of the booklet *How to Usher* by Parrott, published by the Zondervan Publishing House.

IV. CONCLUSIONS

From Genesis through Revelation worship occupies a central place in the life of God's people. There is coming a day when our earthly worship will culminate in the true worship of the "lamb that was slain from before the foundations of the world." The theme of worship is dominant throughout the Book of Revelation as it speaks of the future glories for each believer in the unceasing enjoyment of heaven (Revelation 7:9-17). We should prepare now for that eternal worship by learning the significance of the lesson Christ taught the woman of Sychar, that of worshiping God in spirit and truth.

ASSIGNMENTS

1. Discuss the meaning of worship. Show how this applies to both personal and corporate worship.
2. Discuss the difference between the Old Testament and the New Testament concepts of worship.
3. Discuss the differences between the evangelical concept of worship and concepts held by other groups.
4. Discuss the difference between the objective and the subjective approach in worship.
5. Prepare what you would consider an ideal order of service for a worship service, showing the songs, activities, details to be indicated in the bulletin, etc.

ADDITIONAL READING

1. *A Historical Approach to Evangelical Worship* by Ilion T. Jones. Published by Abingdon Press.
2. *An Outline of Christian Worship* by Maxwell. Published by Oxford University Press.
3. *Music and Worship in the Church* by Lovelace and Rice. Published by Abingdon Press.
4. *The Endless Song: Music and Worship in the Church* by Kenneth W. Osbeck. Published by Kregel Publications.
5. *The Fine Art of Public Worship* by Blackwood. Abingdon-Cokesbury Press.
6. *The Public Worship of God* by Henry Sloane Coffin. Published by Westminster Press.
7. *The Way of Worship* by Brenner. Published by MacMillan Press.
8. *Worship* by Evelyn Underhill. Published by Harpers.
9. *Worship in the Churches* by McNutt. Published by Judson Press.
10. *Worship — the Christian's Highest Occupation* by Gibbs. Published by Walterick Printing Co.

INDEX

190